The Cockroach Trilogy

Three plays by

Nano Riantiarno

The Cockroach Trilogy

Three plays by

Nano Riantiarno

Translations by
John H McGlynn and Barbara Hatley

and an introduction
by Barbara Hatley

LONTAR

Jakarta, Indonesia

Contents

Introduction

Teater Koma, arguably Indonesia's most productive and successful theater company—with an astounding 225 productions between the time it was founded and the date of this book's publication—celebrated its 45th anniversary in March 2023. This publication was originally intended to celebrate the achievements of Teater Koma, but with the passing of its leading co-founder and director, Norbertus "Nano" Riantiarno (June 6, 1949–January 20, 2023), it also commemorates Riantiarno's vital contribution to Indonesian dramatic history.

What Koma has achieved in fact is unique in the history of modern Indonesian theater, that is, scripted plays on the Western model rather than traditional forms of theater. Developing with the impact of European cultural influence from the 1920s and '30s onwards, modern Indonesian theater became the pursuit of a small circle of Western-influenced, internationally-oriented intellectuals, students and artists. Even after a move away from European models, a rapprochement with indigenous performing styles, and a broadening of its social base in recent years, performances are attended by people with a specific interest in theater. Koma's productions are reminiscent instead of performances by the best indigenous popular theater troupes, touring the country, staging a different story each night, mixing dialogue with music, dance and slapstick humor, aiming above all at attracting and entertaining audiences. The similarity is not fortuitous; Riantiarno spoke with admiration of the dynamism and spontaneity of traditional Indonesian theater, which he first encountered in his hometown of Cirebon, on Java's north coast, and then consciously studied during six months of travel through the country in 1975, spending time with numerous regional troupes. He found great strengths in traditional theater, particularly the intimate rapport created between actors and audiences. In his own work he has tried to combine something of the general spirit of indigenous theater, rather than any specific formal qualities, with European dramatic models, in particular, that of the musical.

Riantiarno cited as a precedent and an inspiration for his blending of Western and Indonesian dramatic traditions the spectacular "Malay Opera" of the early twentieth century (c. 1910–40), an amalgam of European, Middle Eastern and Malay elements. Mary Zurbuchen writes that such theater emerged with the rapid modernization and urban growth of the late colonial period in Indonesia. Its hybrid style and repertoire were calculated to appeal to ethnically diverse urban populations with time and money to spare for entertainment. Teater Koma's success has been in turn closely connected with a more recent surge of economic growth and urban development, most spectacularly in Jakarta. Like its "Malay" predecessor, Teater Koma's audiences are drawn from an expanding and ethnically-diverse urban populace. In the current era, impressive growth has occurred in the burgeoning middle class. And, if judged by such measures as clothing and transport, it appears that large numbers of people of this class are attracted to Teater Koma performances.

These facts are commonly used as a basis to characterize Teater Koma as very much a phenomenon of contemporary, capitalistic Indonesian society. The group's colorful and entertaining shows, catering to the tastes of the affluent middle class, are seen to exemplify trends towards commercialization and commodification. Though this characterization has some factual basis, it shows only part of the picture, for the fact is that this is yet another, crucial, way in which Teater Koma's plays make reference to their social environment.

The three plays translated in this volume, *Time Bomb* (*Bom Waktu*), *Cockroach Opera* (*Opera Kecoa*) and *Julini's Opera* (*Opera Julini*), share the same setting and cast of characters. Through their songs and colloquial language and raunchy humor, they illustrate admirably a blending of the energy of indigenous folk expression and the style of a Western musical. The mixture creates a kaleidoscopic presentation likely to appeal to sophisticated urban audiences. But these plays, with their graphically literal representation of the dark "underside" to elite prosperity, subvert rather than affirm middle class assumptions.

On the set of *Time Bomb*, directly below the chairs of a group of oblivious restaurant diners (class-compatriots of the play's viewers), sits a slum on the banks of a fetid canal where the victims of Jakarta's transformation into a rich urban center play out their struggle with life. The officials whose role it is to clear the slums and to expel their inhabitants—in the name of "progress" and "development"—are depicted as corrupt, weak, and hypocritical individuals who are constantly uttering fatuous statements wickedly reminiscent of real-life government-speak. Meanwhile, the speech and action of the slum-dwelling "cockroaches"—prostitutes, transwomen, and thugs, as well as hardworking newcomers to the city—is tough, lively, and down-to-earth. Riantarno brings the "cockroaches" from the banks of the fetid canals so the affluent middle class can no longer ignore them. He lets them tell their own stories which are dramatic, tragic but also told with humor and song. As Agus R. Sarjono remarks in his introduction to *Trilogi Opera Kecoa*, the Indonesian version of *Cockroach Opera Trilogy*, audiences "laugh uproariously but suddenly we realize that our hearts have been seriously wounded and drenched in tears." (*Terus terbahak-bahak hingga kita tersadar bahwa hati kita diam-diam sudah terluka parah dan bersimbah airmata.*)

For all their humor and fun, these performances are not "mere entertainment," but rather purveyors of a stinging critique of the social injustice found in the "real world" just outside the theater doors. They are faced with a choice: continue to ignore the struggles and suffering of the cockroaches or take action to change their lives. We do not know that the influential and high-placed people who return home laughing from Koma performances, in reflective moments, also weigh their own actions and social responsibilities against the social critique of the plays, but we can hope.

Riantiarno explained the place of social criticism in his plays in terms of a necessary connection between living, engaging, up-to-date theater and its social context. Such theater reflects contemporary society in all its aspects, including its conflicts and problems. In conversation, the playwright would often shake his head ruefully over a current political scandal, then excitedly expound on his plan for reference to this issue in a future production. And amazingly, in the highly-charged, repressive atmosphere of Soeharto's New Order Indonesia (1965–1998), where threat of closure hung over newspapers engaging in overly-frank reporting, and performances, films, and television were heavily censored, Teater Koma was able to present such critique quite freely. It wasn't until May 1989 that trouble began when *Sam Pek Eng Tay*, Teater Koma's rendition of a popular Chinese-based tale, was refused permission for performance in Medan, North Sumatra. Ethnic and political sensitivities, compounded by Riantiarno's own Chinese background, presumably gave rise to the ban. Despite the ban, Teater Koma continued its cheeky critique of Indonesian social norms. In early 1990 the troupe presented *The Buriswara Conglomerate* (*Konglomerat Buriswara*), a spoof on the dealings of Indonesia's labyrinthine business cartels, and, later that same year, *Succession* (*Suksesi*), a satire about a supposedly ailing old king and his family, an unmistakable reference to the most sensitive of political issues in Indonesia: presidential succession.

At the beginning of 1991 Nano announced that he was withdrawing from performance for some time, perhaps two years, to rethink his troupe's direction. Riantiarno must have decided that he had more to contribute by speaking out than by keeping silent because, in late 1991, Teater Koma was already back on stage, this time with *Insane Asylum* (*RSJ*/*Rumah Sakit Jiwa*), a story of doctors who are taught that it is better to keep their patients docile, muttering phrases in unison, then to encourage them to recover their normal thinking powers. Any parallels with life outside the theater were, of course, up to viewers to interpret. And Teater Koma has continued to perform until today. Indeed, Teater Koma has now staged 225 productions along with frequent TV appearances. Then, in 2019, came the time of the dreaded COVID-19 pandemic. Thereafter—no live shows, no audiences, everyone in lockdown. But Teater Koma continued to perform "virtually," and audiences could watch their shows at home. A particular highlight was Riantarno and Ratna performing together as husband and wife in *Love Token (Tanda Cinta)*.

Now with Riantiarno's passing one might fear some uncertainty about Teater Koma's future. But in the words of key troupe member Budi Ros, in keeping with its name, Teater Koma, meaning comma, but no pause, "Teater Koma will continue, with Mas Nano within our spirit, eternally."

Barbara Hatley

References

Agus R. Sarjono. "Urban Poor Opera," in Nano Riantiarno: *Trilogi Opera Kecoa*; Yogyakarta: Mahatari, 2004.
Budi Ros. Personal email communication February 13, 2023.
Nano Riantiarno. Personal conversation, 1983.
Zurbuchen, Mary. "The Cockroach Opera: Images of Culture and Development in Indonesia," in *Tenggara,* Vol. 23, 1989.

I
Time Bomb

Translated by Barbara Hatley

Author's Dedication:
For my son, Bangkit Sentosa, who came, then left,
as a ray of light, shunning the world to choose eternity, instead

Main Characters

ROIMA, a young tough
JULINI, a transsexual, Roima's "girlfriend"
JUMINI, a woman who has lost her husband and child
KUMIS, a civil defence guard
BLEKI, another civil defence guard
ABUNG, a mad philosopher who lives in a tree
TARSIH, a pretty and popular prostitute
KASIJAH, another prostitute
TURKANA, Jumini's companion and admirer
TIBAL, a young villager newly arrived in the city
TUMINAH, Tibal's sister
SAWIL & BILUN, a pair of dreamers & schemers
SUBDISTRICT HEAD, a government official
SECRETARY, the secretary to the Subdistrict Head

Other Characters

A SINGER
PROSTITUTE 1
PROSTITUTE 2
FIVE DINERS
OTHER PROSTITUTES
OTHER TRANSSEXUALS
GUARDS

Production History

Time Bomb was first staged and performed by Teater Koma at Taman Ismail Marzuki, the Jakarta Arts' Center, in September 1982. The play was first published in Indonesian also in 1982.

Introductory Scene

Night. A bright moon shines. Beneath a well-lighted bridge, a row of huts stretches along the river and into the background. The slum's inhabitants dream of a better life. JUMINI, a young woman who has lost her husband and child, stares at the moon. ABUNG, a crazed philosopher who lives in a tree, appears to be sunk in thought. At the window of a cheap hotel, a would-be SINGER practices. On a higher level, above this panorama, is a fancy restaurant. Five DINERS, people of apparent wealth, are seated at a table. They eat their dinner, almost statue-like, without speaking.

JUMINI: (*Staring at the moon*) You smile down every night. Why don't you come here? Come to me. I know you miss me. I miss you, too, constantly. On a bright moonlit night like tonight, I know you must be out, playing. And your father, lying on the bench in front of the house, is singing Javanese songs and thinking of me. (*She pauses and as she does TURKANA, JUMINI's friend and admirer, enters without a word*) Smiling down every night.... What news would you bring if you came down to meet me? No, please don't bring me bad news. I don't want bad news. Who would?

(ABUNG *looks up at the sky. The* DINERS *greedily eat their dinner. The* SINGER *prepares to sing.*)

JUMINI: But you never come. Never... I wish I could cut you down from your hanger in the sky, if only for a moment, to hold you in my lap and ask you about my little boy. Would you tell me that he's fine? I don't want a sad answer. Who would?

But all you do is smile. Every night, just smile...

(ROIMA, *a good-looking young man, suddenly emerges from the hut he shares with* JULINI, *his transwoman girlfriend.*)

ROIMA: (*Angrily*) You're ugly Julini, and mean! You don't care about me anymore. You're used up; worn out!

(JULINI *comes out of the same hut in pursuit of* ROIMA.)

JULINI: As if I care! Take my bra, my hair piece, my ass...

ROIMA: And I'll throw them in the river!

JULINI: You wouldn't dare! Thief!

ROIMA: Putting me off like that.... Why shouldn't I be angry?

JULINI: Well, you trying to force me like that when I'm tired. Who'd put up with that? My bra, my hairpiece, my backside...

ROIMA: I swear I'll burn them.

JULINI: You're a sadist. I'm clearing out.

ROIMA: I'll take a razor to them!

JULINI: I'm going, I tell you, I'm going.

ROIMA: Big deal. You think I can't find me another slut? Hell, there's a warehouse full of sluts like you in the world.

JULINI: Is there really?

ROIMA: So, go if you want.

JULINI: Honestly?

ROIMA: It's up to you.

JULINI: Is that it?

ROIMA: (*Even more angry*) Every night—it eats me up: my heart, my soul—holding in my feelings, pacing up and down like I've nothing to do, swallowing my spit.... When can I spit it out? Every night, I feel my blood rising. My muscles tense—Medicine don't help—my hands begin to itch and tingle, just waiting for someone to punch. Shit! (JULINI *goes back into the hut.*) They say that the more tired you are, the hornier you get. That the harder you work, the more you think of a nice bed with a mattress and pillows. But washing the sheets every morning and night—it wears them out. And soap's expensive. Shit! Coconut oil's expensive, too.

(JULINI *comes out of the hut with a bundle in her arms.*)

JULINI: I'm going! I got my bra, my hairpiece, and my ass. That's my capital. Don't try to follow.

(*Swinging her hips as she walks,* JULINI *disappears behind the pylon of the bridge. At first* ROIMA *just stares, stunned that* JULINI *would actually leave him. But then he grows even angrier.*)

ROIMA: Son of a bitch. Alone again! And lonely again. And single again. She's left me again. Julini's gone. She's gone. Help! Julini's gone!

(ROIMA *breaks down and begins to cry uncontrollably.* ABUNG *stares upward. A cloud covers the moon. A group of* BEGGARS, *the slum's inhabitants, crawl out of their huts. The would-be* SINGER *begins to sing in semi-operatic style, his voice clashing with* ROIMA's *moans.*)

SINGER: *In the sky, so many stars,*
And a sliver of moon, peeking
Like a young girl's breasts,
On her wedding night.

(*The* SINGER *keeps repeating the same phrases.*)

JUMINI: (*Angrily*) There's never any peace around here. Roima and

Julini—a cheap love story if there ever was one. A gutter romance, as filthy as they come. To hell with your love-making. I hope your bum swells and your whozee-what's-it bursts with boils. When will I get some peace? (*Going into her hut*) If you died and went to hell, who would care?

(*The* SUBDISTRICT HEAD, *a government bureaucrat, enters with his* SECRETARY *and* BODY GUARD. *They stand beside the bridge, looking at the hovels.*)

SUBDISTRICT HEAD: What an extraordinary sight this is. My dear friends, why must you suffer such a fate? To have to live like pigs in dirty hovels along the river. Who must take responsibility for your fate? There is little I can do. I can only survey the scene. I can only look. (*To his* SECRETARY) Handkerchief! Your suffering must end. These awful hovels must be replaced with buildings, apartments and hotels. I will report to the district head, to the governor, to the president, if need be. (*To the* SECRETARY) Tissue! It's extraordinary. This sight is extraordinary! My friends, I swear that I shall fight for you to be able to live a proper life. Secretary!

(*The* BEGGARS *gather around, like dogs.*)

SECRETARY: Yes, Sir.

SUBDISTRICT HEAD: Write this down. This area must be cleaned up, and soon. Everything dirty and disgusting must be swept away. We'll pull everything down. Yes, we'll raze the entire area. Fix me a time to see the governor.

SECRETARY: Yes, sir.

SUBDISTRICT HEAD: (*With trembling voice*) It's extraordinary, an extraordinary sight. If those people up there can close their eyes to your fate, I, your subdistrict head, can not. I will do something. I will pull everything down. We will knock this all down.... (*To the* SECRETARY) Towel!

(*Weeping into his towel, the* SUBDISTRICT HEAD *leaves, followed by the* SECRETARY *and* BODY GUARD.)

BEGGARS: (*In chorus*) Extraordinary! Extraordinary!

(*The* FIVE DINERS *continue to eat their meal, undisturbed.* TURKANA *enters. The* SQUATTERS, *darkened shapes, scramble out of their huts. They mumble and mutter, but it's not clear what they are talking about.* ABUNG, *who is perched on a chair in a tree, stares at the sight below him and begins to sing.*)

ABUNG: *Compare one hundred rupiah*
For a plate of rice
With five million for a birthday gift.

Compare five thousand a month
For a monthly wage
With one million from a ten percent kickback?

My land, my country,
That I love

Compare a hut on the river bank
With a shining palace
In which no one lives.

And feelings of fear, pain and apprehension
With the laughter of victory
After the general elections

My land, my country
That I love
The future, what will it bring?

(*Suddenly there is a sound of gunshots. The* BEGGARS *scream, fall to the ground, and rapidly disperse. The* SINGER *stops singing and closes the hotel window.* ABUNG *looks tired, weary of it all. Another volley of gunshots rings out, this time closer. The* DINERS *continue eating, oblivious to the commotion below. Two civil defense guards,* KUMIS *and* BLEKI, *appear, intending to disperse the crowd, but the* BEGGARS *have already disappeared.*)

KUMIS: Get out! Scram!

BLEKI: They've gone...

(BLEKI *lights a firecracker.*)

KUMIS: From a distance I thought there were lots of people. Judging from the commotion, ten thousand or more. If anything happens here, it's me who gets the blame. It's me who cops the anger and gets the demotion. The security of this area is totally my responsibility.

(*The firecracker that* BLEKI *lit explodes like the sound of gunfire.*)

KUMIS: (*While running, looking for a place to hide*) Get out of here! Go!

BLEKI: (*Chuckling*) Hey, it was only a firecracker.

KUMIS: A firecracker?

BLEKI: Yeah, you know.

KUMIS: I thought it was gunshot. What are you doing, scaring me like that? Damn you!

BLEKI: Might as well go, sir. Seems safe around here. They don't usually have demonstrations in the middle of the night.

KUMIS: You never know. The enemy can sneak in from any

direction, catch you unawares, if your eyes aren't peeled. These huts would make an easy hiding place.

BLEKI: The most you find here at night is crazy Abung up there in the palm tree. Maybe he stole a cassette or something and all the racket you heard was from that. Let's wake up Sawil or Bilun and cadge a cigarette.

KUMIS: Nah, we'd better go.

BLEKI: Yeah, I suppose.

(KUMIS *and* BLEKI *exit. The stage is silent.* ABUNG, *still perched in his tree, looks down on the sight.*)

ABUNG: So many problems. So many problems. You can't choose one and leave the rest. You have to find solutions for all of them. But which one first? I can't work on them all at once. I'll have to think about this; think hard...

(*As* ABUNG *counts silently on his fingers, the lights slowly dim.*)

1

Night. A prostitution complex on the river bank. Only the poles that support the prostitutes' huts are visible. One of the prostitutes is teaching an English class. The TEACHER'S PUPILS *are her colleagues, other* PROSTITUTES. *They appear to be listening to the lesson, if only halfheartedly.*

TEACHER: (*Loudly*) One way to improve your standard of living is to study a foreign language and a foreign culture. You don't want to be satisfied with just being a whore. Who says we can't dream of good fortune coming our way? Why can't we dream of being the wife of a big shot or an official?

FIRST PUPIL: You mean the seventh wife, Teacher?

TEACHER: Seventh wife is still a wife. Your welfare is guaranteed. Now let's go over yesterday's lessons.

(*The* TEACHER *slowly intones the vocabulary items. Her* PUPILS *slowly repeat the words, with a strong Indonesian accent.*)

TEACHER: *Ini sa-pi.* (Pronounced "ee-nee sah-pee")

PUPILS: *I-ni sa-piii.*

TEACHER: This is cow.

PUPILS: This is coowww...

TEACHER: *I-tu sa-pi sa-pi.*

PUPILS: *I-tu sa-pi sa-piii.*

TEACHER: Those are coowws.

PUPILS: Ndose ar koww wes.

TEACHER: *I-ni monyet.*

PUPILS: *I-nii monyeet.*

TEACHER: This is monkey.

PUPILS: Ndiss is mongkiii.

TEACHER: *I-tu ko-dok.*

PUPILS: *I-tuuu ko-dooook.*

TEACHER: That is frog.

PUPILS: Ndat is prooooog.

TEACHER: *I-tu ba-bi.* That is pig.

PUPILS: *I-tuuu ba-biii.* Ndat is pig.

TEACHER: *I-ni kursi.*

PUPILS: *I-niii kursiii.*

TEACHER: Itu kursi. *This is chair. That is chair.*

PUPILS: Ndis is cheer. Ndat is cheeer.

                (*From a distance comes the sound of music.*)

TEACHER: Hey, hey, where are you going?

SECOND PUPIL: We're tired, Teacher.

                (*One of the* PROSTITUTES *begins to sing. Another joins in and is soon followed by the rest. The* TEACHER *seems to be at a loss about what to do.*)

PROSTITUTES: *Butterflies flying by night,*
Shimmer in the light of the moon,
When the sun appears,
They turn into filth.

                (JULINI *enters, grumbling to herself.*)

JULINI: Shit! I've had it. I've had it up to here.

FIRST PROSTITUTE: It's Julini. Julini's here!

SECOND PROSTITUTE: That's funny. She's usually parked down at the night market.

JULINI: My heart feels broken. What the cure is, I don't know.

FIRST PROSTITUTE: (*To the others*) It's Julini. Julini's here!

                (*From below the embankment the* PROSTITUTES *emerge, like crickets from their holes.*)

JULINI: Is Tarsih with a client?

TARSIH: I'm here. What is it, Jul?

KASIJAH: Why do you ask only after Tarsih. Don't you ever think about me?

JULINI: (*Sympathetically*) How could I forget about a friend who shares my own fate?

> (JULINI *begins to sing.* TARSIH *and* KASIJAH *later join in.*)

JULINI: *Forget the wounded heart,*
Forget the tortured soul,
Seeing ourselves mirrored in each other's eyes,
We send our cry to the sky.

TARSIH: *The sky does not care,*
The night remains dark,
And daylight blinds our eyes.

KASIJAH: *But the stars and the moon*
Are faithful friends
In times of loneliness.

TARSIH: *And the night wind*
Forever begs us
For our body and our soul

JULINI: *Let the sky be dark,*
Or blindingly light,
Forget the wounded heart,
Forget the tortured soul,
When we see ourselves mirrored in each other's eyes.

> (*They laugh in agreement.*)

TARSIH: Have you been quarrelling with Roima again?

KASIJAH: You always come running over here when you're having problems with Roima.

JULINI: Where else am I to run to if not here? I'm all alone. I have nowhere else to take my troubles. I am but a dried flower carried by the wind into the ditch water. When will I find a man whom I love and who loves me, who doesn't desire me only for my services? There's more to life than a mattress.

KASIJAH: A bed, you mean.

JULINI: Well, a bed has a mattress, hasn't it? Roima has never understood that I am a very sensitive person. My love for him is as soft as snow. But he's forever hurting my feelings. He knows that I cannot escape his grasp. That whenever I run away, I shall surely return to his arms. It's fate, just fate...

TARSIH: Is Roima so special?

JULINI: Listen, there's no other man who can plow like my Roima. He is rough but gentle, forceful but giving. He might have a ready fist, but he also has an easy caress. If you speak of water, Roima's a waterfall. Of wood he is teak, of fruit he is a mango. In short, he's the best. Oh, I miss him so. I thrill at the thought of him. I must go back.

(JULINI *exits hastily.*)

KASIJAH: She's mad.

TARSIH: She's in love.

(KUMIS *and* BLEKI, *enter, intending to find* TARSIH *but she spots them before they see her.*)

TARSIH: (*To* KASIJAH) Oh, it's them again. They want the lot but never want to pay. Say I'm booked up.

KASIJAH: Who is it? Kumis and his dog?

TARSIH: Who else? Tell them, will ya?

(TARSIH *hurries off.*)

KASIJAH: (*To the audience*) In this game you'll find many people who demand a lot but who don't want to give a thing. Parasites is what they are. Fine-looking perhaps, but dangerous.

FIRST PROSTITUTE: (*To* BLEKI) Inspection, love?

SECOND PROSTITUTE: Coming down to look us over, love?

BLEKI: Have there been any problems? Have you heard of any trouble?

FIRST PROSTITUTE: It's all quiet, here. It certainly ain't raining money tonight.

BLEKI: Raining money? Crap!

SECOND PROSTITUTE: Not crap, doll. But there is a distinctive smell.

FIRST PROSTITUTE: Maybe it's just Galunggung, erupting again.

BLEKI: Joking with officials, are you? Always playing around, never serious.... What do you think this is? A picnic? When I ask you a question, I expect a straight answer. If we took you in to headquarters then you'd know.

KUMIS: (*Softly, to* BLEKI) Stop beating around the bush. Ask for Tarsih, stupid. You're wasting time with your yapping.

BLEKI: Yes, boss! (To KASIJAH) I'm looking for the flower among flowers. The flower whose perfume spreads for thirty kilometers, the flower far more radiant than the light of the moon...

KUMIS: (*Grabbing* BLEKI) Cut the drivel! Ask them about Tarsih. Don't squirm about like a goddamned worm.

BLEKI: Yes, boss. (*Turning back to* KASIJAH.)

KASIJAH: You looking for Tarsih?

BLEKI: (*Surprised*) Yes. Is she here?

KASIJAH: She just went off with some gents in a limo. She told me that she was booked up.

BLEKI: (*Angrily*) When the boss wants her, she's supposed to be here. Who's the ape who pinched Tarsih tonight? Who's the toad who picked her up? Tell me! (KUMIS *pulls him away.*)

Who is it? Whoever it is, he's had it, trying to compete with a uniformed official. (KUMIS *pulls him off stage.*) Yes, sir. Sorry, sir!

(*As* KUMIS *and* BLEKI *disappear, the* PROSTITUTES *burst into laughter and then begin to sing.*)

PROSTITUTES: *Butterflies of the night,*
Shimmer in the light of the moon,
When the sun comes up,
They change to filth.

(*A cloud covers the moon. The lights slowly fade.*)

2

Morning. Beneath the bridge. JUMINI *is mending clothes. The* DINERS *in the restaurant above relax at their table, enjoying coffee and desserts. The sun glows gently.* TURKANA *is sorting cardboard.* ROIMA, *who is still angry with* JULINI, *approaches her and pulls her by the ear.*

JULINI: Don't, Roima. Please? Don't do that to my ear. Owww!

ROIMA: Where were you last night? Tell me.

JUMINI: You're always so mean to Julini. How can you treat your girlfriend like that?

ROIMA: You keep out of it. This is a private matter. (*To* JULINI) Where did you sleep last night? Tell me, bitch, or I'm going to...

JULINI: (*In pain*) Oh.... Give me a chance! You don't have to hit me.

ROIMA: Tell me then.

JULINI: I didn't sleep anywhere. I was at the station, walking up and down. I feel stiff all over from the cold air and the night

	wind. I'm sorry, Roima. I'll make it up to you. Let me kiss your lips...
ROIMA:	Who do you think you are, staying out like that? And coming back here, like some rich bitch, thinking everything will be fine. Well, up yours, whore!
JULINI:	Don't say that. I'm not a whore. I'm not a wanton woman who likes to wander and stray. I'm just a poor, wretched, woman. Oh, God, take pity on this poor soul who is all alone in the world! (JUMINI *starts to laugh.*)
ROIMA:	It's not funny. (*But he starts laughing, too.*)
JULINI:	(*Happily*) You see. I do know how to keep you entertained! Love me, Roima! Love me with all your heart.
ROIMA:	How am I supposed to love you when you're off peddling your ass?
JULINI:	Don't joke around. I'm not just a piece of merchandise. I'm a PTS graduate, you know, with a diploma to boot.
JUMINI:	PTS? What's that? A Private Technical School?
JULINI:	No.... A "Purveyor of Tenderness and Satisfaction"!
ROIMA:	So, with me, too, it's just a trade?
JULINI:	Not with you, Roima. With you I've found true love. Only with you have I no interest in trade. Only with you am I carried away on a sea of passion.
ROIMA:	Bullshit! Get out of here. You sound like a trashy novel. All I'm saying to you, is that if you come back, don't run off.
JUMINI:	In any relationship it's not unusual to have bedroom problems.
ROIMA:	Get out of here!
JULINI:	Don't you want a kiss first?

(ROIMA *pulls* JULINI *away towards a concealed spot.*)

ROIMA: Come here...

(JUMINI *smiles. The lights change. A spotlight shines on* ABUNG, *who is sitting in a tree and dangling his legs.* ABUNG *looks around him, and then crawls from one position to another. The only sound is that of the* PROSTITUTE-PUPILS *learning English.*)

TEACHER: *Ini monyet...*

PUPILS: *I-nii monyet.*

TEACHER: *Itu mo-nyet mo-nyet.*

PUPILS: *I-tuu mo-nyet mo-nyet.*

TEACHER: This is monkey, that are monkey.

PUPILS: Diss is mongkiii, dat ar mongkii.

TEACHER: *Ini babi, itu babi-babi.*

PUPILS: *Ini babiii, itu babi-babiii.*

TEACHER: This is pig. That are pigs.

PUPILS: Diis iss pig. Dat ar pigesss.

TEACHER: *Ini kursi.*

PUPILS: *Iniii kursiiii.*

TEACHER: This is a chair.

PUPILS: Diss is a cheeer.

TEACHER: *Itu kursi-kursi.*

PUPILS: *Ituuu kursi-kursiii.*

TEACHER: That are chairs.

PUPILS: Daaat ar cheeer-es.

TEACHER: Remember: chairs. Remember: chairs.

PUPILS:	Remember chair, remember chairs.

(*As the* PUPILS*'voices fade,* ABUNG *addresses the audience.*)

ABUNG: During the day our problems turn into sweat and evaporate in the sun. At night, beneath a blanket of moonlight, they become more complex and intertwined. And sleep is not a constructive escape, but, rather, a postponement of the burden we must bear. What in fact are our problems, our difficulties, the things that stand in our way? They're ubiquitous, lurking in every corner, ready to stab us as we go by. It's no wonder we feel confused and helpless.

(*The spotlight on* ABUNG *fades. The lights change again.* JULINI *emerges from the place where* ROIMA *dragged her. Her clothes are disheveled.*)

JULINI: That wasn't a kiss—that was rape! That man! He has no sense of time or place. He just goes wild. I'd have thought he'd want something else to eat in the morning!

JUMINI: My husband was like that too.

JULINI: But Roima's a real man, I'll give him that. Comparing him to a farmer, his tilling is skillful and exact. That's what makes me love him to distraction. The only trouble is, he doesn't want to marry me legally.

JUMINI: But can he? Is it allowed?

JULINI: No barrier can stand in the way of true love. (*Sighing*) Oh, this is my fate: to be a mere object of desire.

JUMINI: Don't let it get you down. Just keep on trying.

(SAWIL *and* BILUN *appear, busy counting their imaginary profits.*)

SAWIL: One kilogram of meat is two thousand rupiah. Cooking oil and kerosene, another five hundred...

BILUN: Wouldn't it be better to use wood?

SAWIL: There's too much waste, and the smoke gets in your eyes. That might put customers off. So how much was that—one thousand five hundred? The oil will last for two or three days. Then there's vegetables, onions, chili and noodles... Let's say an outlay of five thousand for the lot. But that's not counting the initial capital for the stove, benches, plates and cups. How much do we charge per bowl? A hundred?

BILUN: At least.

SAWIL: Okay, a hundred. But we should have a two-hundred-fifty portion, too.

BILUN: Yeah, with two pieces of tofu and five meat balls. And thick noodles instead of thin ones.

SAWIL: We could make nine thousand in a day.

BILUN: That's if we sell out...

SAWIL: Well, at the very least, seven thousand. That a two-thousand profit! But that's the worst case. Let's say two thousand five hundred.... How much is that a week?

BILUN: Seven days to a week so two thousand five hundred times seven is...

            (SAWIL *scratches the figures on the ground.*)

SAWIL: Two thousand five hundred times seven is—seventeen thousand five hundred! And per month?

BILUN: Multiply by thirty, eh, I mean four.

SAWIL: Times four is... seventy thousand!

            (*As* BILUN *and* SAWIL *do their calculations, they move farther and farther away from* JUMINI *and* JULINI.)

SAWIL: A year?

BILUN: Multiply by twelve.

SAWIL:	Twelve times seventy thousand.... Seventy times twelve is eight hundred and forty, with three more zeros.... That's eight hundred and forty thousand. (*Exiting*) Almost a million!
BILUN:	We could buy rice land.
SAWIL:	Rice land and a car. In a year, two years, three years if we save carefully, we could...

(*Their voices fade away. For a moment the stage is silent.*)

JUMINI:	Everyday, all they do is count...
JULINI:	And dream of selling noodles...
JUMINI:	Dreaming, constantly dreaming.
JULINI:	And tomorrow they'll have a different dream. Buying land in Lampung, maybe, and selling cloves. The day after, they'll be dreaming of something else: trading in building materials. And the next day, opening a coffee shop. The following day, selling off the gold from the National Monument. They're crazy!
JUMINI:	They never stop.
JULINI:	Even though they don't have a cent to their name.
JUMINI:	They're sick.

(*As the lights change,* JUMINI *is left in shadow but the restaurant where the* DINERS *are eating remains bright.*)

JUMINI:	Smiling down, every night.... Why don't you come to me? Come down. Please.... How long must I wait?

What's he doing now? Asleep already? Surely, by this time he must be sleeping soundly. I hope his father hasn't forgotten to cover him and to light a mosquito repellent coil before he goes to sleep. His skin will be eaten up by mosquitos if his father has forgotten.

Smiling away up there.... Have you taken note of everything that's happened? What do you have to tell me? I want to know everything about him, and about his father, too. When are they going to come and get me? Didn't he tell you? Why not? Of course.... He has lots of work to do, especially if he's getting ready to come and fetch me. I'll be so happy when he takes me home. But you never say anything. All you do is smile. (*Angrily*) What are you staring at me like that for? Why don't you say something? Do something!

(TURKANA, *who is looking on, says nothing. The lights fade.*)

3

Same location. JUMINI *is sewing,* TURKANA *is sorting cardboard. By their tone of voice, they appear to have been talking for some time.*

TURKANA: I keep telling you that remembering what's past is useless. You've said yourself that daydreaming is like being addicted to drugs. It can make you sick. But what do you do every day?

JUMINI: I wait for Sueb and my boy to come home and get me.

TURKANA: Jumini, Jumini... Sueb and Tole are dead. I brought the newspaper, you saw the news. Their ship sank. Lots of passengers drowned.

JUMINI: (*Angrily*) Sure, lots of them drowned, but I didn't see a picture of Sueb and Tole. They weren't there! They're in Lampung, growing cloves and rice. And when they have enough money saved up, they're going to come and get me.

TURKANA: There's a list of the dead. Where is that paper? You still have it, don't you? I'll show you their names.

JUMINI: Sueb and Tole are common names. You don't know if it's Sueb, my husband, or Tole, my boy.

TURKANA: They're dead, and it's just our bad luck that we weren't able to see their remains.

JUMINI: They're alive! Don't talk about their "remains" like that!

TURKANA: I'm sorry, but I have to, otherwise you're going to spend your whole life in a daze. I don't want you to end up like Abung, sitting up there, dangling his legs in a tree every day, made crazy by his own thoughts. I don't want you to be like Bilun and Sawil who can do nothing but count. Why they'd count the hairs in their armpits if they could. And then there's Roima, and Julini, who dreams of becoming a woman. I want you to see the truth. Sueb and Tole are dead!

(TURKANA *pauses, waiting for a response from* JUMINI *but she remains as still as a statue. He continues, wearily.*)

For almost a year I've been screaming for you come to your senses. But it doesn't seem to do any good. (*Hopelessly*) Oh, well, do what you like...

(TURKANA *exits. The lights change again.*)

JUMINI: You're still smiling. Do you see what I want to see? Sueb and Tole miss me, don't they?

(*The lights fade. The* DINERS *greedily eat their food.*)

4

The local guard house. KUMIS *and* BLEKI *have two visitors,* TIBAL *and his sister* TUMINAH, *who have just arrived from the village.*

KUMIS: Life in Jakarta is hard.

BLEKI: It's not easy.

KUMIS: Even those with jobs have trouble getting by.

BLEKI: Not to mention those who don't have work.

KUMIS: It looks easy, sure. There are lots of jobs waiting, everywhere. And you can make money as long as you're willing to use your brain a bit, exert your muscles.

BLEKI: Do whatever you can.

KUMIS: But to survive in Jakarta? Hmmm…

BLEKI: You have to be able to take hard knocks.

KUMIS: Don't sell yourself too high.

BLEKI: Cut your prices.

KUMIS: Do whatever you can, just so long as it brings in money.

BLEKI: If you're in a spot, you can steal, too—as long as no one catches you.

KUMIS: (*Nodding at* TUMINAH) What's her name?

TIBAL: Tuminah.

BLEKI: Pretty, eh?

KUMIS: She's your sister?

BLEKI: Your real sister?

TIBAL: Yes. It says so in the letter from the village chief if you don't believe me.

KUMIS:	We believe you.
BLEKI:	Sure, we believe you.
KUMIS:	(*To* TUMINAH) Have you ever been to school?
BLEKI:	State, private or religious?
KUMIS:	(*Exasperated*) Shut up, you fool! I asked her, not you. Go sit in the corner over there and shut your mouth, permanently if possible. You just can't let anyone else talk.

(BLEKI *shrinks at* KUMIS' *rebuke.* KUMIS *paces the floor.*)

TIBAL:	This is how it is, sir. We have a letter from our village chief and we have letters from the ward chief and the neighborhood head giving us permission to cultivate some of the unused land alongside the river. We're hoping to grow vegetables, but the ward chief and the neighborhood head told us to speak to you first. So, whatever you say is fine with us. As for the profits.... Those can be divided, too, however you say. Maybe four ways: between you, me, the ward chief and the neighborhood head...
KUMIS:	So you want to be...
BLEKI:	An urban farmer!

(KUMIS *moves towards* BLEKI *as if to strike him.*)

BLEKI:	(*Pleading*) Don't, please don't. I'll be quiet.
KUMIS:	Good! (*To* TIBAL) Good! You are like the morning sun, full of light and hope. Jakarta is becoming barren and all we can see these days are shacks, rubbish, trees, skyscrapers and monuments. But vegetables? You only see vegetables in the market. Here, amid the snarling traffic of this city, you want to become a farmer? Why not a bus conductor, a parking attendant, or a night watchman?
TIBAL:	I only know how to farm.

KUMIS: Well, that's good, a noble profession. Most of us come from the village and most village people are farmers so most of us are farm children. We often forget it, though. Keep on with your plans, keep on. (*To* TUMINAH) And what's your name again?

TUMINAH: Tuminah.

KUMIS: And you want to be a farmer, too?

TUMINAH: I'll do whatever my brother does.

KUMIS: You don't want to be a waitress, a sales clerk or a nightclub hostess?

TUMINAH: (*Demurely*) All I know is the soil.

KUMIS: The soil.... From earth we come and to earth we shall return. So, keep on with your plans. My prayers go with you.

BLEKI: Amen.

            (BLEKI *titters. Suddenly, a hotel window is thrown open. The* SINGER *sticks his head out and begins to rehearse a semi-operatic song.*)

SINGER: *In the sky, so many stars,*
            And a sliver of moon, peeking
            Like a young girl's breasts,
            On her wedding night.

            (KUMIS *covers his ears, trying vainly not to hear the* SINGER's *discordant song but the* SINGER *keeps repeating the phrases.*)

KUMIS: (*Angrily*) Bleki, where did that creature spring from? Shut his trap. This is the age of the atom, the Rolling Stones, the Beatles.... What's he singing that kind of crap for? Plug his mouth. That noise gives me a headache.

(BLEKI *throws a rock at the hotel window.*)

BLEKI: Shut up, you old crow. Shut up!

SINGER: (*Offended*) Primitive savages. No idea of art.

(*The* SINGER *disappears from sight, slamming the window shut.*)

KUMIS: Art? You call disturbing the peace art? Shit! You've got no shame.

(*The* SINGER *reappears at the window.*)

SINGER: With art, the more disturbing the art, the higher the quality. Didn't you know that? *Ben je gek?*

(*The* SINGER *disappears again, this time slamming the window even more loudly.*)

KUMIS: What the hell did he say?

BLEKI: It was Dutch, sir. He said you're mad.

KUMIS: (*Angrily*) What? I'll have the neighborhood chief close down that hotel, that den of iniquity. I'll burn it down myself if I get the chance. Swearing in Dutch... Are we still a colony? I intend to report this to the Subdistrict Head, the District Head, the Governor...!

(KUMIS *falls back, exhausted.*)

TIBAL: Sir, sir...

BLEKI: He's out of it. Just let him be...

(TIBAL, TUMINAH, *and* BLEKI *stare at the recumbent* KUMIS. *The lights fade.*)

5

Late afternoon, a few days later. TURKANA *is counting his cardboard boxes.* JUMINI *is sewing while* ROIMA *and* JULINI *smooch.* ABUNG *moves, ape like, from one tree to another. Up above the* DINERS *enjoy their meal.*

ABUNG: The world is getting more and more full of crazy people. And they're the ones who make it! Those who aren't crazy never get anywhere. If you want to be part of the act, you got to be crazy or stoned. But however fortunate the crazy ones may be, the pious are still the better off.

JUMINI: (*Loudly to* ABUNG) If everyone were mad, the word "mad" wouldn't exist. Come down out of that tree, Abung. You're going to turn into a bird if you stay up there much longer.

TURKANA: You're wasting your breath. He doesn't understand anything. He doesn't hear anything, and he doesn't see anything.

JUMINI: Like the moon, which night after night can only smile.

TURKANA: Don't start that again.

JUMINI: I started long ago. I can't stop now.

(TURKANA *keeps silent.* JUMINI *says no more.*)

JULINI: They're always fighting—just like us—even though I know that Turkana loves Jumini.... He loves her to distraction. Supposing he were asked to jump down a well for her, he'd do it. Oh, if you were like Turkana, how happy I would be.

ROIMA: You're not satisfied with me?

JULINI: Completely satisfied. You're everything to me. If you are Zeus, I am Leda. We will go everywhere together, traverse hell if that is...

ROIMA: Stop! Your blather gives me a headache.

(TIBAL *and* TUMINAH *enter, returning home from their field.*)

JULINI: Are you just getting home?

TIBAL: Yes.

JULINI: You must be tired.

TIBAL: Yeah...

JULINI: I bet you'd like a massage.

TIBAL: If it didn't cost anything, sure.

JULINI: I'm good at massage.

ROIMA: (*Slapping his hand across* JULINI*'s mouth*) You rotten flirt!

(TIBAL *and* TUMINAH *go into their hut.*)

JULINI: Now what's the matter?

ROIMA: Your talk, that's what! You go too far.

JULINI: They're good neighbors. What's wrong with being friendly? We're all newcomers here, trying to make a living in a strange land.

ROIMA: Friendly is fine, but you don't have to advertise. (*Pulling* JULINI*'s ear*) Want this?

JULINI: Ouch!

ROIMA: Or this?

JULINI: Ouch, ouch!

ROIMA: Everything's for sale! Prices will be slashed. Or maybe you want this...

(JULINI *runs towards her hut, followed by* ROIMA.)

JULINI: It's still daylight, Roima! People will see us.

ROIMA: Shut up, slut. All your yelling, people are going to hear.

(*Inside the hut,* JULINI *begins to giggle. A short while later, the hut is silent.* SAWIL *enters, followed by* BILUN.)

SAWIL: Ten rupiah times.... Well, say at worst, ten tins. If one tin holds twenty liters, that makes two hundred. So how much is that?

BILUN: That would be ten times two hundred.

SAWIL: Two thousand! So, in a week: two thousand times seven. That makes fourteen thousand. A month—fourteen thousand times four. And for a year, multiply by twelve.... Hmmm, that's not very much.

BILUN: I told you, there's not much profit in selling kerosene. A lot less than selling noodles.

JUMINI: (*To* SAWIL *and* BILUN) Hey, you two. What are you counting every day?

SAWIL: Profits.

JUMINI: You want to go into business? Do you have any capital?

BILUN: I said, why don't we see how much we can make by from selling rolls. There's no hassles in that. You have your profits plus a commission and monthly wage from the bread factory.

SAWIL: Okay.... One roll costs...

BILUN: Two hundred at least. That's a fifty rupiah profit. There's four hundred rolls in a load so if you can finish two loads in one day.... Well, you work it out.

JUMINI: I asked you, do you have any capital or not?

(SAWIL *does his calculations on the ground.*)

SAWIL: Fifty times four hundred times two...

BILUN: Plus five hundred a day for commission and fifteen thousand a month for salary...

> (SAWIL *and* BILUN *gradually make their way towards the river bank.*)

SAWIL: Five hundred times thirty is fifteen thousand. With another fifteen thousand that's thirty thousand. And if you...

> (SAWIL'*s voice fades away but* JUMINI *continues to speak to them as if they were listening to her.*)

JUMINI: (*Irritated*) So do you have any capital or not? (*To herself as much as to* TURKANA) Those two drive me mad.

TURKANA: You're never going to get an answer from them. You're just wasting your strength. Why don't we leave this place, Jumi? We can go back to the village. I still have two squares of rice land there. We could cultivate that. Better that than waiting here, getting nowhere and fooling ourselves.

JUMINI: Everything makes me sick. Everything! Those two. You, too. You say you love me, that you want to do what I want, that you want to help, that you won't ask me to go back to the village before I've tired of this game of ours. You say this and that.... Why can't you be patient?

TURKANA: All right, Jum, all right.

JUMINI: You say you accept the situation, that you won't ask for anything, that you'll look after me until I die, that you don't care what I do as long as we're together.... Have you forgotten all that?

TURKANA: But we've been lying to ourselves. We'll go mad if we go on like this.

JUMINI: I don't care, as long as you don't betray me.

> (JUMINI *goes into her shack.*)

TURKANA: Listen to me, Jum. I haven't finished yet.

(TURKANA *tries to follow* JUMINI *into the hut, but she pushes him back out.*)

JUMINI: You try coming in here one more time and you'll never see me again.

(*Turning her back on* TURKANA, JUMINI *goes back inside.*)

TURKANA: (*Angrily*) What do you want me to do? Keep begging on my knees to you forever? Do you think I can stand that? Damn, damn, damn!

(*The lights fade.*)

6

Night. The prostitutes' complex. The PROSTITUTES *are having an English lesson. A number of* TRANSWOMEN *are visible, too. In the restaurant, one of the* DINER*'s chairs is empty.* JULINI, *who is sitting in on the English lesson plays with a large doll, a duplicate of the missing* DINER, *during the lesson.*

PUPILS: Dat are piig.

TEACHER: This is *kerbauuu.*

PUPILS: This is *kerbauuu.*

TEACHER: English is a language of communication, an international language. We as workers in the field of social services must serve all nationalities and races, without distinction. It is important that we know English, so that we don't get cheated. Isn't that right?

PUPILS: Yes, Teacherrr.

(*Out of sight, behind the embankment,* TARSIH *can be heard, arguing with* KUMIS.)

TEACHER:	Now try to sing the song I taught you yesterday. Ready?
PUPILS:	*Baa, baa, black sheep* *Have you any wool* *Yes sir, yes, sir three bags full.* *One for my mother,* *And one for my dream,* *But none for the little girl* *That cries in the lane.*

(*TARSIH's quarrel with* KUMIS *grows louder.*)

TARSIH:	Promises, nothing but promises! Do you think I can live on promises?
KUMIS:	It's just for tonight. I'll give you four times the price tomorrow. I don't have any money now.
TARSIH:	Tomorrow.... Always tomorrow! How many tomorrows have there been already?
KUMIS:	Why don't you trust me? This is me, Kumis!
TARSIH:	I've had enough!

(*The sudden noise of something breaking is followed by the sight of* KUMIS *scrambling up the embankment in nothing but his underwear. He ducks into an alley and is followed by* BLEKI, *who scurries behind him with his uniform.*)

BLEKI:	Wait! You can't run about naked like that. People will think you're a thief. Your uniform. I got your uniform. What do you want me to do with it? Sell it to the rag man?

(BLEKI *follows* KUMIS *into the alley.* TARSIH *appears.*)

TARSIH:	(*Angrily*) You come here again and I'll cut it off!
KASIJAH:	(*Giggling*) I didn't hear you complaining before.
TARSIH:	He caught me; I couldn't get out of it.

KASIJAH: That is our lot. If you're not lucky you're really out of luck.

(TARSIH *and* KASIJAH *sing of their sorrows.*)

TARSIH & KASIJAH: *One loaf of bread is all you got,*
Bite off a little today,
But leave some for tomorrow.
My mouth is very strong,
My tongue knows how to dance,
Get drunk, forget it all.

I am a goddess with night for a shawl,
My lipstick, the light of the moon
Hoping that the stars will fall
On the canopy of my bed.

I am a goddess without hope,
The mist which instantly disappears,
The rainbow screened by the sun,
The foamy waves, a loaf of bread.

Take a little bite, just one bite
But leave some for tomorrow.

JULINI: (*Playing with the doll*) One night I saw him, a god descended from the sky. He waved his hand, supple but strong. I went up to him and.... It was truly amazing! What woman would not have fallen in love with him? My eyes swam just looking at him. "Do you want me?" I asked. He smiled. "Are you so special?" he asked. "Try me," I said. "Is it real or only plastic?" he then asked. "Is it important?" I asked in return. "What's important is pleasure," I told him. "It is an art," I convinced him. And we went off. Drinking, dancing cheek to cheek...

(JULINI *embraces the puppet and sings.*)

Oh devour the night,
Turn out the lights
And time becomes glue
Fusing love and desire.

Pleasure, isn't that what we seek? Money is secondary.

(JULINI *moves the puppet then begins to dance.*)

To find a real man on the course of life,
Is to seek a needle in the grass,
So if you ever find him,
Dare not, never let him go.

But as soon as he was satisfied, he left. It's always like that. They come and go like dandruff.

(*Music plays as* JULINI *dances a farewell dance with the doll. When the dance is finished, she throws the doll up to where the* DINERS *are seated. One of the* DINERS *catches the doll and places it in the empty chair. He then returns to his own chair and continues his meal, as if oblivious to what has just happened. Below,* JULINI *cries as she sings.*)

Good-bye pleasure,
Once and for all,
Hello pain and loneliness,
My greetings as we meet again.

(*The lights change leaving* JULINI *in darkness.* TARSIH *and* KASIJAH *are caught in a beam of light,*)

TARSIH: Julini is right. We never get anything out of life. It's our lot always to give. But how long can we go on giving? Even the sea can run dry.

KASIJAH: But what else can we do?

(TARSIH *shakes her head, but a moment later looks up. She seems to have discovered something.*)

TARSIH: Why not? What makes us different from those people up there who do nothing but eat? And don't want to do anything else, even though they could? What makes us different from those who have eyes but who cannot see? From those who have mouths but will not talk about our fate? Who have brains but will not use them to think? Who have power to change their surroundings but are content to sink in their own mire?

KASIJAH: Are you all right, Tarsih?

TARSIH: I'm fine. I just want us to be able to do something to change our lot.

KASIJAH: How? Take up weapons? The only weapon we have is our honor.

TARSIH: Honor? When we spend our whole lives wallowing in the gutter, how can we talk of honor? The longer we go on the less of it we have.

KASIJAH: Everyone wants to be happy, I know that. Everyone wants a proper life. I know that, too. Who wants to live like us? No one—that is, if they have any choice. But everyone knows, too, that we're one part of something immoral. To talk of changing the situation, that's nonsense. The only thing that's going to change the situation is a miracle.

TARSIH: A miracle, Kasijah. That's it. Why can't we make a miracle with our own hands. I can. I can. (*Singing*)

Rise up, maggots,
Why let yourselves be tied to dreary days?
Don't give up, maggots
Why let your burdens weigh you down?
In the sky, the stars and the moon,
Their light shining in the distance,
Shall become our guide.

Don't let yourselves be wounded, maggots
Why are you willing to suffer?

We really are maggots, Kasijah, born in filth.

(TARSIH *runs off towards the main road, followed by* KASIJAH *in swift pursuit.*)

KASIJAH: Tarsih! Tarsih! Tarsih!

(*The lights die quickly.*)

7

Night. JUMINI *is arguing with* TURKANA *outside of her hut.* ABUNG, *in the trees, moves from one perch to another. The* DINERS, *in their place, resolutely enjoy their dinner.*

TURKANA: Why don't we go back to the village? Sueb's land is lying idle. Mine, too. No one is working it. There's no purpose to us living here. What are we waiting for?

JUMINI: What are we waiting for? What am I here for? Why? Who, oh who? Who is he? Who am I?

TURKANA: I just don't know what to do any more.

ABUNG: Thrown up here with no explanation at all, what am I supposed to do? What am I? A character? A character with no discernible role. What tale shall I enact? When should I perform and when should I rest in the wings? (*Angrily*) I'm tired, so tired, but I can't stop. So many people are allowed to live without any preparation, none at all. Their souls cry out. They bump into each other. Some are wounded and bleeding. People queue up to find out what they think can make their life happy.

But the queue doesn't move, even as more and more people step into line. Demon credit presses for payment of our debts.

TURKANA: Answer me, Jumini, answer me! You don't want me to leave you, do you? When I ask you outright, you won't answer me.

(SAWIL *and* BILUN *suddenly appear.*)

SAWIL: Who would want to go it alone? In business, partners have to go along with the agreed policies, even if the venture goes bankrupt. That's the risk of the trade. If you're not lucky then you're unlucky.

BILUN: I only said, how about if we stopped counting. If you don't agree, fine, we'll keep on counting.

SAWIL: Well praise be if you really understand. Shall we start again?

BILUN: Fine.

SAWIL: Where were we?

BILUN: A chicken costs a thousand rupiah.

SAWIL: Which we can sell for twice as much. At a busy market we could sell, maybe, fifteen a day. How many is that in a week?

BILUN: Multiply by seven.

SAWIL: Fifteen times seven is one hundred and five. In a month— four times one hundred and five is four hundred twenty.

BILUN: Less transportation, meals, bribes...

(*The two slowly moving offstage as* SAWIL *does his calculations in the dirt.*)

SAWIL: Four hundred twenty.... Two meals a day, to economize. One meal is four hundred so two people makes eight hundred. Times thirty.... Plus zero, zero is twenty-three...

BILUN:	Is twenty-four.
SAWIL:	Twenty-four thousand! And transport costs?

(*Their voices fade.*)

TURKANA: Look at them, Jum. Look at what they're doing. What do Sawil and Bilun want? They count things that don't even exist. Sure, Sueb and Tole are alive. Sure, they've gone to Lampung, but...

JUMINI: Shut up Turkana, shut up! I don't want to hear what you're saying, not anymore. Go wherever you like and don't bother me.

(*The hotel window suddenly opens and the* SINGER *begins to sing.*)

SINGER: *And a sliver of moon, peeking*
Like a young girl's breasts,
On her wedding night.

(*Just as suddenly the* SINGER *closes the window again.*)

TURKANA: (*Exploding in anger*) This place is a torture worse than hell. This isn't the place for us. I'm amazed that you can stand it at all.

(TURKANA *exits angrily.* JUMINI *looks up at the moon in the sky.*)

JUMINI: Smiling again, are you? Forever smiling. Tonight your light is especially bright. But starting tomorrow you'll begin to shrink and, gradually, fade away. And I'll have to wait another month to look into your face and to ask about Sueb and my boy. On nights when it rains and the sky is covered by clouds, you don't appear and I cannot help but be upset. Even so, I know that you'll be back to smile at me.

(*The moon clouds over. The lights slowly fade.*)

8

Night of the same day. In the opposite corner of the stage from Jumini's hut, JULINI is massaging TIBAL. TUMINAH is seated beside her.

TIBAL: (*In pain*) Ouch, not so hard. It hurts, you know.

JULINI: Well of course it hurts. If it's pleasure you want, don't come asking for a massage. Ask for something else.

TIBAL: Hush. Ah, there, that's where it hurts. I must have pulled a muscle.

TUMINAH: (*To* TIBAL) I can do that for you.

TIBAL: That's all right. You must be tired. Why don't you go to bed.

(TUMINAH *rises and enters the hut.*)

JULINI: My, she an obedient thing.

TIBAL: I know. She never talks back. I'm her mother and father, two in one. It's hard looking after a young unexperienced girl.

JULINI: You mean, she's never even...

TIBAL: I tell you, when she gets married, I'll feel the loss. I hope she finds a good husband. He doesn't have to be rich, as long as he's responsible. That's enough for me.

JULINI: How are your crops? They must be big by now.

TIBAL: In another few weeks it will be time to harvest. We should be able to make a tidy profit.

(TUMINAH *looks out of the door of the hut.*)

TUMINAH: You'll buy me a nice dress, won't you?

TIBAL:	Yeah.... And if there's enough, we'll put aside some for your marriage.
TUMINAH:	No need for that. Buy me a necklace or earrings. If we're out of money we can sell them.
TIBAL:	It's late. Go to sleep. Otherwise you'll wake up late. The middlemen who are going to buy our crop said that they'd be here first thing in the morning.

(TUMINAH *goes back into the hut.*)

JULINI:	How much are you bribing Kumis?
TIBAL:	Not bribing—sharing the profits. That's the arrangement.
JULINI:	Don't trust Kumis. He only looks after himself. Be careful.
TIBAL:	Yeah, yeah.... Ouch!
JULINI:	Oh my God.... It's standing up.
TIBAL:	What?
JULINI:	It's stiff.
TIBAL:	What are you talking about?
JULINI:	It's going up and down.
TIBAL:	Shhh...
JULINI:	I know a place where we can go. Do you want to? It's nearby.
TIBAL:	I don't have any money.
JULINI:	Money's secondary. What's important is pleasure.

(JULINI *and* TIBAL *sneak off to a darkened corner. A moment later* TUMINAH *appears and gazes in the direction Julini and Tibal have gone.* ROIMA *appears.*)

ROIMA:	Jul... Julini! Where has that whore gone? Jul, where are you?

Turning tricks, I bet. You said you wouldn't do it today. (*To* TUMINAH) Have you seen Julini?

(TUMINAH *nods in the direction* JULINI *and* TIBAL *have gone, then enters the hut and shuts the door.*)

ROIMA: Hey, don't go in yet. Tell me where she went. Who was she with? Say something, idiot!

(ROIMA *walks off in the direction indicated by* TUMINAH.)

ROIMA: Juul...

(TUMINAH *silently reappears at the door of the hut. The lights slowly dim.*)

9

Night. The prostitutes' complex. The SUBDISTRICT HEAD, *his* SECRETARY, KUMIS *and* BLEKI *are making an incognito inspection of the area. As on previous occasions the* PROSTITUTES *can be seen preening and showing themselves off.*

KUMIS: No need to worry, no need to be nervous—our subdistrict head doesn't take advantage of people. He's a wise official with the people's interests at heart, especially those of the little people, the underdogs. He's here because he wants to learn about your line of work. When he interviews you, please give honest answers. The material he gathers will be forwarded to his superiors. As this is not an official visit, you're not being asked to behave officially. Our subdistrict head regards this prostitution complex as the most orderly. So, it's appropriate for him to visit.

(*Some* PROSTITUTES *whistle, others giggle.*)

BLEKI: Quiet, quiet.... Be polite. This man's a government official. (*To* KASIJAH) You, step forward. Yes, you.

FIRST PROSTITUTE: (*Whistles*) Kasijah's got a booking!

KASIJAH: Hush.

BLEKI: The subdistrict head would like a few words with you.

KASIJAH: Fine by me.

BLEKI: Go ahead, sir.

SUBDISTRICT HEAD: What's your name?

KASIJAH: Caroline.

                  (*The* FIRST PROSTITUTE *whistles again.*)

FIRST PROSTITUTE: Rubbish, she's making that up.

SECOND PROSTITUTE: Her name is Kasijah, sir.

KASIJAH: Hush...

SUBDISTRICT HEAD: How long have you been working here?

KASIJAH: I'm just in from the village, just three months ago.

FIRST PROSTITUTE: (*Laughing*) Hell, she's the oldest whore here.

KASIJAH: (*To* FIRST PROSTITUTE) Don't spill the house secrets. Don't be a pain in the ass.

SUBDISTRICT HEAD: And how did you come to be like this?

KASIJAH: Like what, sir?

SUBDISTRICT HEAD: Well, like this...

FIRST PROSTITUTE: Being a whore is hard work.

KASIJAH: (*Losing her patience*) Damn you, slut. You smell like the gutter, with a drain for a mouth. I'm going to scratch your eyes out, pull out your hair till you look like Kojak.

(KASIJAH *goes to strike the* FIRST PROSTITUTE *but is stopped by* BLEKI.)

BLEKI: That's enough. I'll shoot you if you don't calm down.

(KASIJAH *and* FIRST PROSTITUTE *calm down but their mutual hostility remains apparent.*)

SUBDISTRICT HEAD: Try another one, Kumis.

KUMIS: Another one.... Hmm, which one? (*Trying to choose.*)

(*Noticing* TARSIH, *the* SUBDISTRICT HEAD *whispers to* KUMIS.)

SUBDISTRICT HEAD: I like that one.... She's really pretty.

KUMIS: (*Nervously*) She's the star, sir.

SUBDISTRICT HEAD: All the better. What's her name?

KUMIS: Tarsih.

SUBDISTRICT HEAD: Call her over here.

KUMIS: (*To* TARSIH) Hey, you, come over here. The subdistrict head wants to talk to you.

TARSIH: (*Swinging her hips as she walks towards him*) Want some action?

KUMIS: (*Taking* TARSIH *by the hand*) Sshh, be a bit respectful.

TARSIH: Take your dirty hands off me. If I start talking about what you're up to, then you'll know about it.

KUMIS: Little bitch.

SUBDISTRICT HEAD: Do you want to be this kind of woman, Tarsih?

TARSIH: Hey, you know my name!

SUBDISTRICT HEAD: (*Embarrassed*) Yes, er, yes I do.

KASIJAH: Read it in the newspaper, I suppose.

TARSIH: Well, I guess we are pretty well-known.

FIRST PROSTITUTE: (*Laughing and pointing at the* SUBDISTRICT HEAD) He's the subdistrict head, now don't go pulling his willy... I mean, his leg!

TARSIH: Stop that, you're embarrassing the man.

SUBDISTRICT HEAD: But seriously, don't you think about your future, Tarsih?

TARSIH: (*Resentful*) I don't have a future. Everyone knows we here don't have a future. It's only people of your sort who have futures. (*In declamatory style*) Prostitutes of Jakarta, unite!

SUBDISTRICT HEAD: Do you really think that's true?

TARSIH: Yeah, it's true. You work hard and you might get a promotion. But us? The older we get the fewer clients we have. We pay taxes, too! We work our guts out, rocking this way and that, while Kumis here and people like him keep demanding payments in kind. And say we want to quit, what are we going to do?

SUBDISTRICT HEAD: There are lots of other types of work. In factories, in offices.... A pretty woman like you doesn't have to work like this.

TARSIH: And supposing we weren't here, how would people like Kumis get their rocks off? Men like that...

KUMIS: (*Muttering*) Me again, me again. What have I done wrong?

TARSIH: I was told to tell the truth. Now I answer truthfully and you get offended.

SUBDISTRICT HEAD: All right, all right.... (*To* TARSIH) Can you speak English?

TARSIH: If I could, do you think I'd be in this place? With English I could charge more, maybe work out of a fancy hotel. It'd be a heck of lot nicer, a lot less hassle, than it is here. That's for sure. Around here you and your kind are always picking on us—those of us without power—the weak—people without connections.

SUBDISTRICT HEAD: I'll make a note of that. Your plight will be looked into. Just be patient...

TARSIH: (*Angrily*) So what's the use of you coming here, inspecting us? Give us a proper job and you're damn right we'll stop being whores. But don't just talk and make inspections. It's noted, you'll look into our plight.... Bullshit, all of it!

KUMIS: We'd better go sir. It's getting a little hot here. If anything happens, I'll get the blame.

SUBDISTRICT HEAD: Your plight will be looked into...

(*The* SUBDISTRICT HEAD *and his party leave. Whistles accompany their departure. A spotlight remains on* TARSIH *alone.* TARSIH *begins to sing.*)

TARSIH: *They always come here,*
Pretending to care,
While waiting for their chance.

They keep on coming,
But only make wider,
The gap that separates us.

For what do they come?

(*Lights return to normal.*)

KASIJAH: Don't let it get you down. We did our best and said what we wanted to say. Maybe it won't work, but at least we got our feelings off our chest.

TARSIH: It just makes me so mad.

KASIJAH: Mad? You aren't mad. You're just doing what you have to do.

TARSIH: But I don't feel right.

KASIJAH: (*Sympathetically*) Don't worry about it. You'll be yourself soon. (*Two people in veils enter and come their way*) Look at those guys, Tarsih. They're probably looking for you.(*One of the two* VEILED FIGURES *approaches* TARSIH.)

VEILED FIGURE 1: Got some time?

KASIJAH: What's it to you if she does?

VEILED FIGURE 1: I'm talking to her, not you

KASIJAH: Well, I'm speaking for her.

VEILED FIGURE 1: What are you? Her pimp?

KASIJAH: Get out of here.

VEILED FIGURE 1: If you're not, keep your mouth shut. She can answer for herself. Are you available or not? If you are, my boss here wants you. And if he's satisfied, you won't have to worry about how much he pays.

             (*Swinging her hips as she goes,* TARSIH *proceeds down the river bank.*)

TARSIH: (*Looking back*) Come on.(VEILED FIGURE 1 *whispers something to* VEILED FIGURE 2 *who nods and follows* TARSIH. VEILED FIGURE 1 *then squats on his haunches at a slight distance from* KASIJAH.)

KASIJAH: And what about you?

VEILED FIGURE 1: Leave me alone.

KASIJAH: What are you anyway, a nurse, wearing a veil like that?

VEILED FIGURE 1: One more word and I'll punch you.

(KASIJAH *restrains her temper and lights a cigarette but then approaches* VEILED FIGURE 1. *When* VEILED FIGURE 1 *is not looking,* KASIJAH *whips off his veil. Both* TARSIH *and* VEILED FIGURE 1 *are surprised.*)

KASIJAH:　　It's you, the subdistrict head's secretary. And the one who went down there is...

VEILED FIGURE 1/SECRETARY: I'll get you...

(KASIJAH *starts to run away, followed by the* SECRETARY.)

KASIJAH:　　If you're the secretary, the other one must be... the subdistrict head!

VEILED FIGURE 1/SECRETARY: Damn you, I'll get you!

10

Same night, different place. JULINI *and* TIBAL *are cuddling.*

JULINI:　　A sliver of moon in the sky, smiling at us, as if to bless our new-found love.

TIBAL:　　You're so romantic.

JULINI:　　There are no clouds, only stars. The water of the river gleams like gold. Nothing can disrupt our intimacy.

TIBAL:　　It's like poetry.

JULINI:　　Our love will be eternal, united like the moon and its beams. You're the first real man I've met. You know what I want? You're my Gatotkaca, my Arjuna, my Superman. Our love will shine forth forever.

TIBAL:　　But look at the moon. It's dark now, covered by a cloud.

JULINI:　　A cloud?

(ROIMA *creeps along in the darkness towards* TIBAL.)

TIBAL: Maybe it's going to rain.

JULINI: Don't leave me. I'm afraid of being alone. If you were to leave, to whom would I turn? Roima is iron but you are gold. Roima is a nasturtium but you're an orchid. Roima is a vulture but you're an eagle.

                (*Unable to listen any more,* ROIMA *jumps out of his hiding place.*)

ROIMA: Well, the vulture is here, looking for dead meat. Where's the corpse?

JULINI: (*To* TIBAL) God help us! Your feeling was right. (*To* ROIMA) Forgive me, Roima, forgive me. Don't hurt him.

ROIMA: Who said anything about hurting him? I want you to go home.

JULINI: No way, not if you're going to be so rough.

ROIMA: Now, girl, go! I've been looking all over for you.

JULINI: Only if you promise you won't hit him.

ROIMA: Why should I? The one on the make was you, not him.

JULINI: So, you're going to beat me up?

ROIMA: Not here.

JULINI: Well then, I don't want to go home. I'm still free to do as I want. We're not husband and wife yet, are we? We're not bound to one another. If you want to find another dude, or another chick, I won't object.

ROIMA: Then what do you want?

JULINI: Marry me and I'll be faithful forever.

ROIMA: We'll talk about it at home.

JULINI: But what do you think about getting married?

ROIMA: I told you, slut, we'll talk about it at home. And if you won't walk on your own two feet, I'll drag you there. It'll make a nice show for the kids around here.

JULINI: No, I won't go.

ROIMA: You've got to. (*To* TIBAL) And as for you, slime ball, don't try moving in on Julini again. She's not yours to move in on.

TIBAL: Whose she? Yours?

ROIMA: That's none of your business, bastard. Do you want to fight about it?

JULINI: Stop! I'll come home.

ROIMA: That's better.

               (JULINI *flees in a panic.*)

JULINI: (*To herself*) Damn the luck, having a thug for a boyfriend.

ROIMA: (*Shouting*) One more time, and I'll show you what trouble is.

               (ROIMA *exits.* TIBAL *sits, thinking.* TUMINAH *enters.*)

TUMINAH: Tibal...

TIBAL: Oh, you're here.

TUMINAH: I was worried that something might have happened to you.

TIBAL: Been here all along?

TUMINAH: Mmmm.

TIBAL: Let's go home.

               (TUMINAH *and* TIBAL *exit, one following the other. The lights slowly dim.*)

11

Night. The prostitution complex. KUMIS, TARSIH, BLEKI *and* KASIJAH *are present.*

KUMIS: You're always saying no. Do you have a new boyfriend?

TARSIH: What business is it of yours?

KUMIS: I've got money now. I can pay my old debts twice over and give you whatever price you ask.

TARSIH: I don't need your dirty money.

KUMIS: How do you know it's dirty?

TARSIH: Because it's from the sweat of other people's labour, that's why. You've no right to it. You sit twiddling your thumbs all day and rake in the cash.

BLEKI: Just take her, boss. What's she going to do about it?

TARSIH: If you try to force me, I'll report you to the subdistrict head.

KUMIS: Oh, so he's one of your clients now, is he? How can I possibly compete?

KASIJAH: That's right. How indeed?

BLEKI: Shut up when the boss is talking.

TARSIH: And supposing he is, what're you going to do about it?

KUMIS: I wouldn't doubt that he is. Just look at his wife, the old witch. After having a taste of you he's not going to go back to that. (*The* VEILED FIGURES—*the* SUBDISTRICT HEAD *and his* SECRETARY—*enter.* KUMIS, *ignoring their presence, continues to talk*) The subdistrict head.... Tell me, can he keep it up like me? Two or three minutes at best and he's snoring. And he has a bad heart, you know. If he had a heart attack, you could find yourself charged with murder. (VEILED FIGURE 1 *coughs*) What are you coughing about? I'm in charge of security here. If I've got business with this woman, you stay out of the way. Or come back later, when I've finished. (VEILED FIGURE 2 *approaches* KUMIS *and lifts his veil to reveal his face. It is the* SUBDISTRICT HEAD. KUMIS *steps back in astonishment*) Yes, sir.

SUBDISTRICT HEAD: I'll see you at my office.

KUMIS:　　　　Yes, sir.

SUBDISTRICT HEAD: Now clear off and don't make trouble.

KUMIS:　　　　Yes, sir. Come on Bleki. It's time for our rounds.

BLEKI:　　　　Who was that, sir? Do you want me to beat him up?

KUMIS:　　　　(*Pulling* BLEKI *along*) Don't argue, idiot. Come along.

　　　　　　(KUMIS *and* BLEKI *exit, accompanied by whistles from the* PROSTITUTES. *The* SUBDISTRICT HEAD *and* SECRETARY *take* TARSIH *by the hand and lead her to her hut.*)

12

Night. KUMIS *and* BLEKI *are engaged in conversation on the bridge.*

KUMIS:　　　　Shit! Blast it! Damn it to hell!

BLEKI:　　　　What's wrong? Do you need my help?

KUMIS:　　　　What am I going to do now? My head feels like it's been hit by a bomb and smashed to pieces.

BLEKI:　　　　Just tell me who did it. I'll smash in his face.

KUMIS:	Maybe I should kill myself, jump off this bridge.
BLEKI:	Wait a minute, sir. It can't be that bad. Tell me what the trouble is. And while we're at it, who was that veiled man? You looked, well, you looked…
KUMIS:	Scared shitless? You bet I was. That was the subdistrict head.
BLEKI:	Lord Almighty!

13

Night. ABUNG *is crouched in his tree, talking to himself and to the sky.*

ABUNG: I am everywhere, present in every event. But what role am I playing now? Am I the lead or just a bit player, present to make the suffering more complete? I know what's going on, but not what to do about it, because that's not in the script. I feel myself outside of events. And after a[space?]while it's no fun being a spectator. (*To the sky*) To whom must I turn to ask? Where? Tell me. Shit, shit, shit…

(ABUNG *moves from one tree to another. Lights dim.*)

14

The subdistrict head's office. KUMIS *and* BLEKI *have come to report to the* SUBDISTRICT HEAD.

SUBDISTRICT HEAD: (*To* KUMIS) Send your guard dog off to the other room. His face gives me the creeps. This is a matter between me and you as my subordinate.

BLEKI: (*Angry but helpless*) All right, I'm going. (*He starts to leave*)

Such is the fate of a subordinate, to always be at the bottom. Come to think of it, being a "sub-ordinate", what hope do we have of getting on top?

(BLEKI *finds a place to sit and gets ready to sleep.*)

SUBDISTRICT HEAD: These are my orders, which you will carry out whether you want to or not: On the first of March, three months from now, the governor is going to inspect this area. He'll be coming here with the district head and the mayor. I've been ordered to clean up this area, and now I am ordering you to clean it up, without fear or favour. Get rid of the squatters' huts, the prostitutes' shacks and the gambling dens. Raze them to the ground. How you do it is your own affair. If you do your job well you might get a promotion, a raise. That's all I have to say.

KUMIS: Yes, sir, but Tarsih's beat is in that area, too, sir.

SUBDISTRICT HEAD: The whole area I said. Don't talk to me about Tarsih. She's not the same Tarsih any longer. She has a whole new outlook on life because of me.

KUMIS: What do you mean, sir?

SUBDISTRICT HEAD: That is none of your business, Kumis. You just carry out my orders. Give the people a couple of months to prepare for the move. Any building without a permit is to be torn down. Understood?

KUMIS: Yes, sir. Um, why is the Governor is inspecting the area?

SUBDISTRICT HEAD: Because it's an important state task. Because.... Oh, how do I know? What I do know is that he's going to make an inspection. Full stop. That's it.

KUMIS: Yes, sir.

SUBDISTRICT HEAD: So, when can I expect you to begin?

KUMIS: As soon as the funds for the operation come through, I'll start right away. There'll have to be feasibility study first and how much that will cost is hard to calculate...

SUBDISTRICT HEAD: Nonsense. You are to get going within a week at the latest. Next Monday I will have your report.

KUMIS: Yes, sir. I'll start at once, sir.

SUBDISTRICT HEAD: Then go. Talking to you makes me feel like I'm on the battlefield, even though all you've got for a weapon is an old hand gun. Off with you.

KUMIS: Yes, sir.

(KUMIS *leaves the* SUBDISTRICT HEAD*'s office. Outside he finds* BLEKI *sleeping.*)

KUMIS: Wake up, you idiot.

BLEKI: Yes, sir. Ready, sir. Where to, sir?

KUMIS: You do nothing but sleep.

BLEKI: Yes, sir. But I wasn't asleep, sir.

KUMIS: Well, what were you doing?

BLEKI: Meditating, sir.

KUMIS: We're going to.... Gad, I get tired of talking to you. It's like being on the battlefield. All that military respect and crap, even though you don't even have a blunderbuss. All you've got is a worn-out stick. Let's go.

BLEKI: Yes, sir.

KUMIS: And shut your trap.

BLEKI: Yes... (*He catches himself from saying more.*)

(KUMIS *and* BLEKI *exit. The lights fade.*)

15

Night. One week later. ROIMA *and* JULINI *are talking in front of their shack.*

ROIMA: We haven't spoken to each other for a week. I've had it. I want to find out what it is you really want. This is wrong, that's wrong.... I can't seem to do anything right. Do you think it's fun for me living under the same roof with a walking statue?

JULINI: If I'm really like that, why do you want me? I told you long ago to give me some kind of commitment. That's all. Do you think I want my fate to hang in the balance like this forever? For you I'm just a picnic basket that you take wherever you go. There's food in that basket, but you never want to eat it. If you leave it too long, I'm telling you, it's going to go bad.

ROIMA: Talk straight, would you? Your allusions give me a headache.

JULINI: But if I tell you what I want, you won't want to do it, so what's the use of telling you what I want?

ROIMA: Before you've said what you want, you're telling me what I won't want. Come on...

JULINI: But you won't want to, I know you won't.

ROIMA: Tell me.

JULINI: You won't marry me, will you?

ROIMA: Who said I won't?

JULINI: Then you will?

ROIMA: Of course.

JULINI: You won't be ashamed?

ROIMA: No.

JULINI: Really?

ROIMA: I swear.

JULINI: Then, when?

ROIMA: It's up to you.

JULINI: (*Moved by emotion*) Oh, Roima, that's the most romantic thing I've ever heard you say. It's like a voice from heaven. You're not fooling me, are you?

ROIMA: Make the arrangements. Find an auspicious day.

JULINI: (*Excitedly*) I'm going to get married! Jumini, Turkana, Sawil, Bilun! I'm getting married! The moon has come down to greet me. I've won the lottery.

            (JULINI'*s shouts wake all of the area's inhabitants. Wedding music starts to play. People put on their best clothes. JULINI is suddenly dressed in a Betawi-style bridal outfit as is ROIMA, who dons a fez and all the trimmings. ROIMA also sports dark glasses, a gold waistcoat and crown. His accessories include a gold belt and sword. The music that accompanies the ceremony is a combination of tanjidor, gambang kromo, disco and dangdut music. The scene is lively as the guests enter to greet the bride and groom. JULINI looks extraordinarily happy but ROIMA seems gloomy. TARSIH comes forward to sing.*)

TARSIH: *A drop of happiness*
            Dissolves without a trace
            In a wallow of filth and pus
            What meaning has a drop of happiness?

            The sky is full of hate
            The sun strikes and attacks

The moon and stars are but distant friends
What meaning has a drop of happiness?

We are moths in the lamp light
Trapped by the certainties of Fate
Which laughs as we flutter and struggle
What meaning has a drop of happiness?

This song of mine is a tuneless song
A song of the rejects
The hopeless and hungry beggars
The bird who pines for the moon

My song is a tuneless song
Tuneless, tuneless, tuneless

(*The* CROWD *joins in.*)

Tuneless, tuneless, tuneless.

(*Fireworks explode.* KUMIS *and* BLEKI *appear. The wedding party continues gaily, spontaneously, until* KUMIS *and* BLEKI *step forward to stop it.*)

KUMIS: Stop it! Stop the party now! I've got good news. Stop the music.

BLEKI: (*While bustling about*) Hey, stop the music. Stop the dancing. I'll shoot you if you don't stop.

(*The merrymaking finally ceases. The* SINGERS *stop singing. Everyone looks at* KUMIS *and* BLEKI.)

KUMIS: It's good luck that you're all gathered here, because I have some good news. The governor is going to visit this area. So, as usual, he wants the area clean. He wants your huts cleared. As long as you have a building permit, there's no need to knock them down. All the rubbish around here has to go. Everything stinking or rotten must go. There will be no compromise because this order comes from the highest quarters!

As the protector of this area, I will try to act kindly. I don't want you to have to move out of here in a panic. I don't want any of the old folks here worrying about a move till they keel over and drop from exhaustion. We have to work together and help one another. You have a month to clean this place up. That's reasonable, isn't it? You can tear down the huts gradually, piece by piece if you want. Where you move is up to you. The main thing is that I've passed on my orders. The rest of it you can work out for yourselves. Understand? Whether you understand or not, do it! Remember, one month. Don't forget. So, go on with the party.

JULINI: (*To* KUMIS) Are you going to let me get married or not?

KUMIS: Oh, this is a wedding party, is it? Who's getting married? You? Who to? This man? Are you all mad, a man marrying a man? Where's the minister? Do you have a marriage license? Hmmm, how very modern. I could take you in for this, you know. You could be charged with creating a disturbance. (*Changing attitude*) But not to worry, not to worry, as long as there's something to, how shall we say, smooth things over. (*Chuckling*) But after that, get out of here. If there's a check from up above, I could get in trouble.

(BLEKI *is given cigarettes and money. He and* KUMIS *help themselves to the food, after which they leave.*)

JULINI: (*Fed up*) The bastards!

(BLEKI *suddenly appears again.*)

BLEKI: Remember, one month!

(BLEKI *leaves. One of the* DINERS *leaves his place at the table to urinate in the public lavatory below.* JULINI *and* ROIMA *sit in dumbfounded silence.*)

LIGHTS CHANGE

JULINI: This could be a bad omen. Just when I start to taste happiness, we're told to leave.

ROIMA: Omen or not, our luck's never going to change.

JULINI: This marriage of ours.... Maybe it's not for the best. You've looked sour about it from the start.

ROIMA: It's just that I realized that, no matter what, you're always going to be a man. Even with a sex change, you'd still be a man. Can your organs be made into a womb? We'll never have children.

JULINI: I know that. But what's the use of torturing yourself? You're still young. Maybe we shouldn't marry.

ROIMA: Maybe that would be better.

JULINI: So, we should separate?

ROIMA: Yes, better to follow our own paths.

(JULINI *begins to cry.*)

ROIMA: There's no need to be sad. That's the way of the world. Nothing is eternal.

JULINI: I know, I know...

(*The lights change again. The* DINER, *having finished urinating, climbs back up to his place in the restaurant. He appears completely oblivious to the happenings around him. The people under the bridge watch his every move. The lights fade slowly and die.*)

16

Night, at the guard house. TIBAL *and* TUMINAH *have come to the guardhouse to see* KUMIS. BLEKI, *who is supposed to be keeping watch, is nodding off.*

TIBAL: You're saying we can't stay here any longer. That's it, isn't it?

KUMIS: That's not what I said. I said the place has to be cleaned up.

TIBAL: Then what about my field? It won't be ready to harvest for another two months.

(*As if not hearing what* TIBAL *has said,* KUMIS *picks up a wad of money.*)

KUMIS: So, this is the deposit? It's all there, no tricks?

TIBAL: Everything is written down. You can check my records if you want.

KUMIS: No, I trust you. (*Handing the money to* BLEKI) Count it.

BLEKI: What's this?

KUMIS: Just count it, don't ask questions. You'll get your ten percent.

BLEKI: Yes, sir. Right away, sir.

(BLEKI *counts the money.*)

TIBAL: (*To* KUMIS) What I'm asking for is a concession. I don't care if our hut has to go, as long as the field is left untouched.

KUMIS: Fine, no problem, as long as there's a kickback. Come here, I'll tell you what I'd like.

(TIBAL *goes up to* KUMIS *who whispers something in his ear.* TIBAL's *face suddenly goes red.*)

KUMIS: There, I knew you wouldn't like it. Well, okay, that's out, but don't think you're going to be able to stay around here any longer.

TIBAL:	(*To* KUMIS) You filthy sack of maggots. (*To* TUMINAH) Come on, Tum, we're going.
	(TIBAL *drags* TUMINAH *out of the guard house.*)
KUMIS:	You got three days! After that don't expect my door to be open. And you can clear off, the whole lot of you.
	(TUMINAH *and* TIBAL *disappear in the distance. The lights in the guard house dims.*)

17

Night. A light shines on TUMINAH *and* TIBAL *as they make their way home.*

TUMINAH:	What did he say to you?
TIBAL:	Shut up.
TUMINAH:	I want to know. What did Kumis ask for in order to let us stay?
TIBAL:	Shut up, I said.
TUMINAH:	I'll shut up if you tell me what Kumis wants. We can work harder if we have to. I don't want to see that field cleared either. We've put too much work into it to let it be ripped up. I'll do whatever I can to prevent that.
TIBAL:	(*Exploding*) He wants you, your virginity, that's what he wants! How could I take that? How could I not get angry? If I'd been alone, I would have taken him on.
TUMINAH:	(*Thinking*) He gave us three days to think about it. I heard him say that.
TIBAL:	Let the field go, he's not going to have you. We can try our luck somewhere else. There's more to the world than this place. You go on home. I'm going to see a friend. Maybe he can give us work.

TUMINAH:	But...
TIBAL:	Go home and get some sleep!

18

Night, a few hours later, at Tuminah's hut. TUMINAH is making herself up to look as pretty as possible. Holding a little mirror in her hand, she puts on lipstick and then, looking into the mirror, begins to sing.

TUMINAH: *For a worm like me*
Is there another choice?

Though what is offered is poison,
Is there any other choice?

All over the world
Arrows are taut in their bows,
Knives and daggers are ready,
Always ready to wound.

Here and there, poison
Is there another choice?
Oh, is there any choice?

(TUMINAH *goes off in the direction of* KUMIS' *place.* BILUN *and* SAWIL *enter quarrelling.*)

BILUN: I'm tired of counting. Counting and counting, all the time. What for? I've just begun to realize it's all for nothing.

SAWIL: If we didn't count what would we do? What can we do besides count?

BILUN: We can stop.

SAWIL: How? When we die, that's when we can stop. Come on, let's count again. How much did you say for a bunch of onions? Three thousand rupiah? Think of it.... If we bought them directly from the farmer for only six hundred, think of the profit we'd make on a truck load.

BILUN: Where's the money, the onions, the truck? Where?

SAWIL: They'll come later. Let's count the profits first. Money can be found. Think of it: a two-thousand rupiah profit just on one bunch. If a truck holds two thousand bunches, that's two thousand times two thousand.

(SAWIL *leaves and* BILUN *is forced to follow. The lights change.* TUMINAH *returns slowly to her hut. The sound of a cane being struck against a metal pole is heard: it is the sound of the night watch.* KUMIS *and* BLEKI *are making their rounds.*)

BLEKI: (*Loudly*) Remember, one month after the announcement these shacks must be demolished. If they aren't gone, they'll be burnt down. (*While walking past* TUMINAH's *hut*) Tum... are you asleep, Tum?

KUMIS: Shut up, big mouth. If Tibal gets his hands on you, then you'll know.

BLEKI: She's quite a girl, isn't she, sir?

KUMIS: Shut your mouth.

BLEKI: It's too bad I didn't get a share of the lower part. Hmmm, quite a girl. (*Loudly*) Remember, you got one month!

(BLEKI *and* KUMIS *exit.* TIBAL *appears and wearily approaches his hut. He looks troubled and sits down outside, in front of the hut. A moment later* TUMINAH *comes out of the hut.*)

TIBAL: (*To* TUMINAH) Aren't you asleep yet?

TUMINAH:	Any luck?
TIBAL:	(*Shaking his head*) I didn't go anywhere in the end. Where was there to go? We don't have any friends. What with the field already planted, I'm out quite a lot. I don't want to see it cleared.
TUMINAH:	It won't be cleared.
TIBAL:	What? (*Suddenly noticing her appearance*) What's going on? You've got your good clothes on and you're wearing lipstick.... Where did you go? Tell me, where have you been?
TUMINAH:	I went to see Kumis.
TIBAL:	You mean you...
TUMINAH:	Yes, I did, and now we won't have to move. After the Governor's inspection we can stay here, build a hut and farm.
TIBAL:	You, you.... (*Screaming*) God damn it! What has all my work been for? For what? For who?
TUMINAH:	Don't worry, it didn't hurt. The important thing is that you can work in peace.
TIBAL:	(*Wearily*) Ours is a rotten lot.
	(*Lights dim.*)

19

The same place. A few days later.

ROIMA:	Yeah, ours is a rotten lot.
JUMINI:	Never have it easy. Always up against it.

JULINI: We try hard but it never seems to get any better.

KASIJAH: A good life.... It always seems far from our grasp. Well, at least Tarsih got out. She won't be coming back.

JUMINI: What do you mean?

KASIJAH: The subdistrict head asked her to be his second wife. No need for her to work anymore. She has a house and money every month. She can have a decent life while we here kill ourselves just to make a cent. And then we have those bastards, always breathing down our necks.

JUMINI: So, what about it Jul? Roima? Have you made up your minds? Gosh, this might be the last time we meet.

(TURKANA, *who is seated off to the side, looks on but says nothing.*)

JULINI: If we don't go what will we do? Yeah, Roima and I are going off together but to different destinations.

JUMINI: Where are you going, Roima? And what about you Julini?

ROIMA: I don't know yet.

JUMINI: We'll miss you.

TURKANA: We'll be scattered everywhere. Where will we all end up?

ROIMA: Are you ready?

JULINI: With steeled heart!

ROIMA: Let's go.

(JULINI *nods. As* ROIMA *and* JULINI *shake hands with their friends the song "Auld Lang Syne" plays on percussion and gamelan.* ROIMA *and* JULINI*'s friend wave their hands in unison as the couple leaves.* SAWIL *appears, counting his steps as he walks.* BILUN, *following close behind, drags along a sack.*)

SAWIL: One, two, three, four, five, seven, nine…

              (*With* BILUN *still dragging his sack behind him, the pair exits. With the exception of* JUMINI *and* TURKANA, *the others leave. The* DINERS *up above relax around the dinner table.* ABUNG, *in his perch in the tree, is reading a book. The* SINGER *appears at the window of the hotel and begins to sing.*)

SINGER: *In the sky, so many stars,*
              And a sliver of moon, peeking
              Like a young girl's breasts,
              On her wedding night.

              (BLEKI *and* KUMIS, *who are still on their rounds, walk past.*)

BLEKI: Remember, you had one month. Now there's one week left. This area must be cleaned up. Remember, one month. In one week, time is up.

              (BLEKI *and* KUMIS *exit. A darkened figure—*TIBAL*— follows them silently, keeping out of sight. For a moment the stage is silent.* ABUNG *then begins to read from the book he holds in his hands.*)

ABUNG: Everyone knows that we have the right to ask. And the right to get a reply. Everyone knows that if we ask questions, it's not because we're trying to light the fires of rebellion. If we ask questions, it's not because we're not loyal. If we ask what our real role is, it's not because we're distrustful. (*Closing the book*) But now, almost no one knows to whom they must address their questions.

TURKANA: It's lonely now. what with Kasijah, Tarsih and the others gone.

JUMINI: There's still Abung and that singer. And Sawil and Bilun pass by now and then.

TURKANA: Another week, Bleki says. What about us?

JUMINI: Does anything have to change? We'll stay here. When the governor comes, we'll tell him what we're doing. If he brings in troops to drive us out, we'll tell them the truth: that we're here to look at the moon. There's no regulation against looking at the moon.

TURKANA: Looking at the moon all the time... aren't you tired of it? Deceiving yourself.... Haven't you had enough? This game consumes our time, our strength, our thoughts. It has to stop.

JUMINI: Tibal and Tuminah are still here.

TURKANA: That's their business.

JUMINI: Well, we have our own business, too.

TURKANA: Looking at the moon? I've had it!

JUMINI: (*Emotionally*) Whatever you want to say, say it. Tell me that Sueb will never come back. That he didn't go to Lampung to raise cloves. That he ran off with another woman and took my baby with him.

TURKANA: Jum...

JUMINI: (*More emotionally*) Do you want to tell me that I'll never be able to forget Sueb? Or that your patience is exhausted? That you're going to leave me just as Sueb left me?

TURKANA: Jum...

JUMINI: Tell me that I have no self-respect, waiting for a man who's taken another woman for a wife. Say it if you want to say it. It's not that I'm not tired. I'm tired too. I don't care about Sueb, but my baby.... He's my boy. Why did Sueb take him from me? I don't want him raised by another woman. I want them to come back.... (*Crying*) I know it's not possible. Of course I know. I don't even know where they are. But the moon knows. She always smiles whenever she appears in the sky. She knows everything that happens on the face of the earth and I ask her. I ask her...

TURKANA: (*Softly*) It's hard for a man not to lose his patience when he keeps coming up against a brick wall. I promised that I would follow you wherever you went. Forgive me. Go on doing whatever you want to do. I won't pester you again.

(JUMINI *goes into the hut.*)

TURKANA: Jum, Jum...

(TURKANA *goes into* JUMINI's *hut.*)

(*The lights slowly dim.*)

20

Night. BLEKI, KUMIS *and* TUMINAH *are inside the guard house. Outside,* TIBAL *lurks in the shadows.* KUMIS *begins to sing.*

KUMIS: *A sad face, a heart full of woe,*
Whatever for?
A perfumed body, satisfying one's needs,
What else could one ask for?
What's the meaning of purity,
If, when the lights go out,
All one knows is pleasure?

KUMIS: Tuminah, Tuminah... your virginity was so precious to you. But when you were with me, in my bed, you were panting just as hard as I was. What took place between us cannot be called rape. You wanted it, too. (*He sings*)

For the first three minutes you rejected me,
For the next three your tongue assaulted me,

I felt myself caught between two hills

KUMIS: (*Chuckling*) Turn out the lights, Bleki, and wait outside.

(BLEKI *appears drunk.*)

BLEKI: Yes, sir. I'm ready for my prize.

KUMIS: The only prize for a dog like you is my drool. (*Spitting*) Now get out.

(BLEKI *leaves the guard house to slump outside the door.* KUMIS *slams the door shut. As the lights fade,* BLEKI *can be heard muttering under his breath.*)

BLEKI: (*In sing-song fashion*) The first three minutes, it was "Oh! Don't! Stop!" But for the next three minutes, "Oh don't stop!"

(BLEKI *chuckles. The lights die.*)

21

Night. The prostitution complex. The complex is deserted, except for KASIJAH, *who is sitting smoking.* TARSIH *enters, looking tired and unsteady on her feet.*

KASIJAH: (*Surprised*) Tarsih! What happened?

TARSIH: There's no rest for people like us. For a while there I thought I could be happy. I had a house and monthly support. But now it's all gone.

KASIJAH: What happened?

TARSIH: The subdistrict head's first wife came to my place with two soldiers and kicked me out. She took everything her husband had ever given me and treated me no better than a beggar. (*Half-singing, half-screaming*)

Hurt, what can I do?
Hurt, that's our lot
Hurt, hurt, hurt.

KASIJAH: I thought it was only me who had a hard time, every day having to drink the piss of lay-about men. But it looks like you've been through it too. (*Laughing*) I can just imagine the look on her face. And she brought soldiers! (*Laughing*) Why not an armored tank?

TARSIH: (*In a normal voice*) Life's never going to change.

KASIJAH: (*Laughing harder*) She pulled out your hair, scratched your face, and screamed that her twat's still clean and her moves still hot.

TARSIH: (*Laughing, too*) Gawd, she looked like a spook. And the way she dressed.... Like Minnie Mouse with a stomach the size of a hippopotamus.

KASIJAH: And she had no teeth. She smelt and her thighs hung in folds...

(TARSIH *and* KASIJAH *sing together.*)

TARSIH & KASIJAH: *Butterflies of the night*
Shining in the light of the moon
When the sun comes up
They turn to filth.

KASIJAH: That's us alright!

(*The two women sit down, wearily.* JUMINI, *too, has apparently decided to move for her bundle of belongings is beside her. She looks wistfully up at the moon.*)

JUMINI: A night talking to you slips by like a passing car. Without realizing it, it's dawn already. We have to leave today. I see, you're not sad. You keep on smiling as if you don't care that one of your friends is going away. The eastern star is beside you and in a moment the sun will come up and outshine your light. I must say good-bye. Turkana says that this little game of ours is useless. And maybe it's true. I'll think about it as he and I travel along.

I know that after I've gone it will be hard to ever find again what we enjoyed this year. Maybe you won't be able to see anymore your face mirrored on the surface of the river. Maybe no one will pester you with questions. No one will care about the beauty of your light. No one, only me.... (JUMINI *begins to cry.* TURKANA *comes up quietly behind her, carrying a suitcase*) In a different place I may not be able to—may not want to—look at you again. Because, I know, it's only here that you can smile. In another place you might cry. I've never seen your tears.

TURKANA: (*Softly*) Don't start again.

JUMINI: Oh, it's time. You're not yellow any more but white. By day you're nothing but a corpse, unwilling to reveal the beauty of your face. Yes, now I'm ready.

TURKANA: That's enough. Dreaming can be sweet but to work is surely sweeter. We'll go back to our village and work. And not because we're defeated.... Because this is not our place.

JUMINI: Alright, I'm ready.

(*The day progresses. From a distance comes the sound of* BLEKI *shouting.*)

22

Morning, outside of Jumini and Turkana's hut. KUMIS *and* BLEKI *are present to supervise the demolition of the remaining shacks.* TUMINAH *remains silent in her hut.*

BLEKI:	We gave you one month, remember. Today time is up.
KUMIS:	There's no need for talk. Just get to work.
BLEKI:	You mean clear everyone out?
	(ABUNG *peers down from his perch in the tree.*)
KUMIS:	Yes, everyone.
TURKANA:	(*To* JUMINI) Are you ready?
JUMINI:	(*Adjusting her bundle*) Yes.
TURKANA:	You knock these places down, Kumis, and I hope you're struck by lightning. Even without you driving us away, we would have left, one by one. How are we supposed to resist our rotten destiny? Jumini and I will go somewhere or other. And sometime, who knows, we might come back.
TURKANA:	(*To* BLEKI) Don't just stare. Demolish these shacks.
BLEKI:	Yes, sir.
	(BLEKI *sets to tearing down the shacks.*)
KUMIS:	(*To* TURKANA) You hate me, don't you?
TURKANA:	Hate you? What for? There will always be people like you. And people like those up there who can only eat, drink, shit and pee. And people like us who are ready to be buried, to become the foundation on which things are built—we, too, will always exist. Why should we hate? We're shadow puppets. What we do is up to the puppeteer.
ABUNG:	(*Shouting*) Like puppets. And I'm a puppet which remains forever in his box, and never appears on the screen. What am I?
TURKANA:	Let's go Jum. If we talk too long, they'll think we're making a speech. Speeches are given by officials, not by nobodies like us. Our duty is to listen.

(TURKANA *and* JUMINI *exit.* BLEKI *approaches* TUMINAH'*s hut.*)

TUMINAH: You're going to tear down my place, too?

BLEKI: (*To* KUMIS) Sir?

KUMIS: Tear it down.

TUMINAH: What about your promise? I gave you what you wanted and you're still going to wipe us out?

KUMIS: I didn't promise you anything. (*To* BLEKI) Tear it down.

(TIBAL *is dragged in by guards.*)

TIBAL: They've torn up our field, Tum.

TUMINAH: And they're tearing down our house!

GUARD: Shut up, idiot, shut up!

KUMIS: Don't stop, Bleki. One down, all down. We can't play favorites.

TUMINAH: But you promised.

KUMIS: I never promised anything.

TIBAL: (*Exploding*) My field is gone. What was Tuminah sleeping with you for? Son of a bitch!

(*The* SUBDISTRICT HEAD, *his* SECRETARY *and several* BODY GUARDS *enter.* TIBAL'*s outburst is quickly squashed.*)

SUBDISTRICT HEAD: Is that man resisting? Arrest him. Put that madman in jail.

(TIBAL, *with his hands tied behind him, looks at them with vengeance.* TUMINAH *cries. The* SINGER *at the hotel window shouts out his song.*)

SINGER: *In the sky, so many stars,*

> *And a sliver of moon, peeking*
> *Like a young girl's breasts,*
> *On her wedding night.*

KUMIS: Jesus, that singer is still here. Tear down that hotel, Bleki. And throw that singer into the river. I'm going to go deaf from his screeching.

(A black cloth falls over the SINGER, *enveloping his body and silencing him.)*

TIBAL: Maybe we can't do anything now, Tum. But later, when the time comes for people like us, then they'll be sorry. I swear they'll regret it.

KUMIS: Regret it? In what way? There will always be army, police and civil guards. Power can move from one hand to another, but police, soldiers and civil guards will always be needed. We will always be here. If I weren't here someone else would be. And in the name of order, guards have a right to act tough. You come here, set up house, and say that all this is yours, that we're not to interfere. What grounds are there to prevent us from driving you out? Take this man away. And the woman, too. Hand her over to the police.

(TIBAL *and* TUMINAH *are taken off.* SAWIL *is counting.* BILUN *drags behind him a sack.)*

SAWIL: One, two, three, five, seven, nine, ten...

BILUN: Sawil, wait for me, Sawil.

(The pair exits. JULINI *enters. She dances and sings for a moment, then begins to cry and laugh.)*

BLEKI: There sure are lots of loonies around here.

ABUNG: (*Exploding*) And now is the moment when I shall find the answers. Who am I? Why am I here? What am I doing here? Why is everyone else given problems and worn away by them while I remain a puppet in the box. Who am I? What am I...

(ABUNG *appears to go berserk and begins to run after the* SUBDISTRICT HEAD.)

KUMIS: He's going off again.

BLEKI: This is bad, sir. Should we shoot him?

(*The* SUBDISTRICT HEAD *screams as* ABUNG *pursues him.*)

SUBDISTRICT HEAD: (*To his* SECRETARY *and* GUARDS) Help! (*To* ABUNG) What are you asking me questions for? I don't have the answers. Ask the Governor when he comes.

ABUNG: The Governor? One of those people up there, who do nothing but eat?

SUBDISTRICT HEAD: The Governor hasn't come yet. What people? I don't see any people up there.

ABUNG: That's right—I must ask the people up there. People who eat a lot are sure to have the answers. You're stuffed! All of you and all you can do is eat. You're hopeless. You've got no guts. Your brains are in your stomach. Stuff it. You won't even answer.

BLEKI: This is getting bad, boss. Do we shoot him or not?

KUMIS: Here's the pistol.

BLEKI: I don't know if I can do this.

(BLEKI *takes the pistol, takes aim. Just as* ABUNG *is about to reach him the gun goes off.* ABUNG *is hit. He starts for a moment, then cries out.*)

ABUNG: What am I? Is this me? Jakarta, Jakarta. Indonesia,

Indonesia.... It's always like that, always like that, but why does it have to be like that?

(*The others say nothing as* ABUNG *dies. One of the* DINERS *turns on a radio.* A RADIO ANNOUNCER'*s voice can be faintly heard.*)

OS ANNOUNCER: Our deepest thanks to those who have made possible the holding of these general elections. With the completion of the elections which have run almost a month in an atmosphere of order, calm, peace, and mutual respect, the outside world will know that we are a country which has successfully carried out our festival of democracy, that we are a country with respect for the rule of law.

(The ANNOUNCER'*s voice gradually fades to be replaced by a pop song.*)

Why do you forget darling
Do you want to remember, darling

(*The same phrase of the song is repeated over and over again. The record appears to be stuck. Final blackout. The curtain falls.*)

THE END

II
Cockroach Opera

Translated by John H McGlynn

Main Characters

ROIMA, a young tough
JULINI, a transwoman, Roima's girlfriend
TARSIH, a pragmatic madam
TUMINAH, Tibal's sister
HIGH OFFICIAL, a high-ranking government official
FOREIGN VISITOR, a foreign investor
SALESMAN, a con artist, a peddler of suspicious wares
KUMIS, a gang leader
TIBAL, a young villager in the city
BLEKI, a gang member
ASNAH, a foul-mouthed prostitute
KASIJAH, another prostitute
MINOR OFFICIAL, a low-ranking government official
BODIGAR, Tarsih's bodyguard

Other Characters

GUARDS
RENT COLLECTOR
PROSTITUTES
TRANSWOMEN
REPORTERS
PHOTOGRAPHERS
STANDERS-BY
CITY MONUMENTS

Production History

Cockroach Opera was first staged and performed by Teater Koma at Taman Ismail Marzuki, the Jakarta Arts Center, in July, 1985. The play was first published in Indonesian that same year.

They are crushed together in gutters and beneath bridges while others play golf.
They yearn for grass while others have excess.
They are merely cockroaches while others are eagles.

1

The stage is bathed in red: the land, the huts, the gutters, buildings, sky, clouds, the sun; even the falling rain. The earth begins to shake and move, and a song, vague and indistinct, rises from somewhere beneath the earth. At moments, the song is a symphony of gongs; at other times, a cacophony of clattering cans. As the song grows louder, the earth begins to heave and mounds of the earth break free from the mother soil to move around on stage with a life of their own. The mounds dance in frenzied motion. The song grows louder and tenser. The earth ripples. Lightning flashing overhead is followed by a roar of thunder. Shafts of light, but not the light of the sun, crisscross billowing clouds of smoke. The song grows louder but is suddenly silenced by a volley of gunfire and then a piercing scream. All that is left is silence and then, moments later, the sound of weeping. Soon the song begins again.

2

ROIMA *enters carrying* JULINI's *corpse wrapped in a while shroud.*

ROIMA: She wanted only to live. She never bothered anyone, never used force. She did what she did because she was hungry. Tell me how else she might have earned some money? Come on, tell me!

Ha, you see; you have no answer. All you can do is talk. Talk, talk, talk. Do you think we can eat talk? She worked, wracked her brains, sweated and slaved to earn a living... And she did earn a living. She was a whore. Yes, a whore. What do you think she should have been? A secretary? All she knew how to do was massage. She was a whore.... Don't think that she didn't have dreams of being a lady tycoon.

But fate threw her into the gutter and had she lived until a ripe old age, that is where she would have stayed, cloistered with the lice and cockroaches. We're nobodies. Our main concern is our stomach. So why was she shot dead? Yes, she was a whore, but look at how many people needed her. So, why was she hunted down and not them, the people who came to her? If you can show us a way to improve ourselves, we'll follow; but not if it's through a gauntlet of guns and bullets.

(The earth trembles and a layer of red earth is violently peeled back. ROIMA and JULINI are dragged together to a bench in Monument Plaza. Before them a split-level panorama appears. The upper level is the silhouette of a silent city, full of buildings and monuments. At one side is a platform, atop of which is a band that stands in wait, ready to play for any occasion. A banner hanging across the platform reads: "The Steel Hat Club Band." The panorama is crowded with monuments: the FRIENDSHIP MONUMENT, *the* PEDICAB MONUMENT, *the* HEROES MONUMENT, *the* SICKLE MONUMENT, *the* HORSECART MONUMENT *and so on. The lower level is made up of houses or, rather, shacks clustered together and joined by low roofs and gutters. There stands a decrepit bridge, a public outhouse and a guard post. There is also a miniature plot of open ground where children might play marbles. The women who are seated in front of their shacks scour one another's hair for lice. Even in this lower half, another division is apparent: on the one side, the house of families, "good" people, and on the other side, a prostitution complex. The daily activities of the complex begin.)*

3

Morning. Monument Plaza. JULINI *awakens on a bench to find* ROIMA *still snoring.*

JULINI: As fresh as morning dew, as fragrant as frangipani flowers…. (*Takes a deep breath and stretches*) It's getting on in the day. (*To* ROIMA) You have to wake up, honey. We have to go before the guards chase us a away. (*Pinching* ROIMA) Honey…

ROIMA: Hey, what's that for?

JULINI: It's late. Are you going to keep on snoring? This isn't a hotel, you know! (*She begins to pack their things.*)

ROIMA: Late? Is it?

JULINI: Believe me for once, would ya. Now where are you going?

ROIMA: I got to piss

(*He urinates by a monument.*)

JULINI: Can't you do that somewhere else?

ROIMA: Like where, for instance?

JULINI: Finished? Come on, tuck it in; let's go.

ROIMA: Just a second…. Hey, if I'm not wrong, our place used to be over there. Look! There's the river, the bridge and Tarsih's place. Where did Jumini's and Turkana's place used to be?

JULINI: (*Putting on lipstick*) Don't know. Somewhere around there, I suppose.

ROIMA: Five years and now it's like this. Amazing! Where are they all now?

JULINI: Dead, probably.

ROIMA: Hush!

JULINI: Well, how am I supposed to know? Why even ask? I can't remember.

JULINI: I bet you haven't forgotten Tibal.

ROIMA: Jealous, are you? Listen, Tibal's past history. Now there's only you, forever...

(*Two* WATCHMEN *suddenly appear in the distance and begin to blow their whistles.*)

What did I tell you. I told you we should go but no, you had to play tourist. Come on!

(*They run off. Strangely enough, the whistles get louder and more numerous.*)

LIGHTS CHANGE

4

Morning. Outside a Jakarta slum. The destitute, the poor, all the "cockroaches" emerge from huts, from shacks beneath the bridge, and from the gutter and, like cockroaches tied together by fate, begin to sing. Two WATCHMEN *look on suspiciously.*

The party is only for those who think of themselves as cockroaches. Only for those who can no longer dream. Only for those who can only yearn for enough food to eat and clothes to wear. Only for those who get by on survival but do not truly live.

Together the SLUM DWELLERS *sing "The Song of the Drunken Roaches."*

DWELLERS: *Hiding in the drainpipes*
Sleeping and eating in gutters
Crawling in the dark
In the dark, my sweet, the dark.

Drunk and dizzy, a headache
Oh, how to deal with life...

(A group of RICH PEOPLE, *walk on stage, line up and sing*
to the crowd.)

Who told you to come to Jakarta
Garbage is all you make
Work hard, start a business
That's the only way to make it here!

Drunk and dizzy, a headache
Oh, how to deal with life...

Everyday you size up the scene
Waiting to seize your chance
Everyday you're thrown back down
To the gutter, my sweet, the gutter.

Drunk and dizzy, a headache
Oh, how to deal with life.

The bellies of the big shots are swollen
What about the bellies of the small?
The share of the big shots is massive
What about that of the small?

Drunk and dizzy, a headache
Oh, how to deal with life...

Oh, the smell of the cesspool
Ulcers, lice and boils, too
That's what we have for our fate
For our fate, my sweet, our fate.

Drunk and dizzy, a headache
Oh, how to deal with life.

(As the song ends, everyone returns to work.)

LIGHTS CHANGE

5

Late night at a prostitution complex. TARSIH *is in the middle of an argument with a* MINOR OFFICIAL *who is flanked by two* GUARDS. BODIGAR, *her own bodyguard, stands by silently in fear.*

TARSIH: This is my house. I have a deed. Why am I being evicted? I'm angry, mad enough to kill!

MINOR OFFICIAL: Calm down. The priorities of the city planning division are beauty and order. You're not being evicted; you're being localized. You'll receive compensation, trust me.

TARSIH: Priorities? Don't talk to me about priorities.

MINOR OFFICIAL: You're not being evicted. You're being relocated. You'll receive compensation. Trust me.

TARSIH: Ha! Trust you? That's a laugh.

MINOR OFFICIAL: Please, think about it. Here we have a whore-house, I mean a "man's entertainment hall" smack dab in the middle of a residential area. There's a mosque and there's a church. Maybe your neighbors haven't said anything yet, but we from the city planning and social affairs divisions have taken note. This complex must be relocated.

TARSIH: We're already on the outskirts of the city.

MINOR OFFICIAL: But the city is growing fast. Sure, maybe you are at the far side now but in a few years—it will feel like overnight—you'll be back in the middle again. The point is, we wouldn't want to be responsible for "negative excesses" at some future date if this complex remains where it is.

TARSIH: For five years now I've lived side by side with my neighbors and there's never been a problem. This complex provides employment opportunities for some of them. Besides, none of our clients comes from this area; they're all from outside.

MINOR OFFICIAL: Nonetheless, Ma'am, I have a job to do and it is my duty to give you fair warning. You still have a while, but you should start getting ready now. Excuse me...

TARSIH: I won't give in. I'm going to stay. This is my place and no one can take it from me. Get out!

MINOR OFFICIAL: There's no need to get mad at me. I'm just doing my job. Good day. (*He and the* SECURITY GUARDS *exit.*) If the people here burn this place down, don't complain to me.

TARSIH: Is that a threat! Bastard!

(BODIGAR *laughs to see the three men go.* TUMINAH *glares at him.*)

And why didn't you say something? You should have chased them away. You got that big moustache of yours but the nerve of a ninny.

BODIGAR: His security boys had handcuffs. I don't like handcuffs.

TARSIH: Next time, if they're not here for entertainment, run them out of here.

(*On the second floor of the complex,* TUMINAH *comes out on the terrace with a client, a* HIGH OFFICIAL.)

TUMINAH: Don't worry, sir.

(*The* HIGH OFFICIAL, *who is wearing only a pair of shorts, is afraid. He shakes with nervousness as he puts on his clothes.*)

HIGH OFFICIAL: Don't call me "sir."

TUMINAH: Alright, honey, but don't be afraid. That was just a mini-drama down there.

HIGH OFFICIAL: Thank God for that. I thought it was raid. I almost had a heart attack. If word got out about me coming here, that wouldn't be good for me. The media would make a production out of it. Where would I be then? (*Turning back to* TUMINAH *in a coy voice*) I'll be back tomorrow, okay? I have some condoms from Japan. We can compare them with those made in Tangerang.

TUMINAH: Get on with you; the sun will be up soon.

HIGH OFFICIAL: Oh, and Tuminah?

TUMINAH: Yes?

HIGH OFFICIAL: What kind of style will you use tomorrow?

TUMINAH: Free style?

HIGH OFFICIAL: Well, not too free. How about the sleeping frog position? I like that one; that one's good for a man my age.

TUMINAH: Fine by me.

HIGH OFFICIAL: And Tuminah...?

TUMINAH: Yes, honey?

HIGH OFFICIAL: You really are something. Tomorrow put me down from 7:00 onwards.

TUMINAH: Sure thing.

HIGH OFFICIAL: Well. I've got to go. (*Singing "The Song of Two Pistols."*)

One pistol, two pistols
One pistol in your hand

The other in your crotch
Mighty heroes go to war
One pistol is fired
Then the other one too
The one smells of powder
The other stains your pants
One pistol, two pistols...

(TARSIH *sits down by herself.* TUMINAH *notices and approaches.*)

TUMINAH: Is there trouble, Tarsih?

TARSIH: You just finish with a customer?

TUMINAH: Yeah, and you know.... (*Whispering*) He's a big shot.

TARSIH: We're going to be evicted. It's just a matter of time.

BODYGUARD: The guy said "relocated."

TARSIH: Ah, get out of here. Go stand guard below.

BODYGUARD: Okay, okay... (*Leaves.*)

TUMINAH: Evicted again? Where are we supposed to go to?

TARSIH: I don't know. I don't want to talk about it and I don't want to hear about it. But we'll do everything we can to stay here.

If necessary we'll take the matter to Parliament. Starting now we have to work even harder and save as much money as we can. It doesn't look like the future is going to get easier.

TUMINAH: It's always that way. Does it ever get easier?

TARSIH: I sweated for this place and I won't have it taken from me. I was a gutter whore long enough and had it up to here with asshole ward chiefs ripping me off. I've been hungry too long and been run out of my home one too many times. This is where I live and this is where I'll die.

TUMINAH: But, Tarsih, who knows, maybe he was a fake, just pretending to be an official. Why else would he come here at night?

TARSIH: No, he was real enough. Had his written orders in hand, signed and stamped, not just a photocopy. He asked for money and I gave him some.... Maybe I didn't give him enough. Then he asked for you but I said you had a visitor. Maybe he got mad for having to wait so long.

TUMINAH: If it's only me he wanted, he could have come here tomorrow.

TARSIH: We'll talk about this tomorrow, Tuminah. God gave us brains to find solutions to problems and now we have to start using them.

(TARSIH *goes inside and is followed by* TUMINAH.)

LIGHTS CHANGE

6

Midday beneath a bridge. A SALESMAN, *who's a bit of a con artist, sets out his wares. A crowd has gathered around him and he speaks to them bombastically.*

SALESMAN: We are a religious people, a people who remember the past and honor our heroes. We are a noble people with noble ideals, a people with incomparable culture. For that reason, dear friends, I would like to talk about cockroaches as I demonstrate to you my magic skills. (*Holding up a picture of something*) What is this a picture of?

CROWD: (*Calling out together*) A cockroach!

SALESMAN: (*Showing another picture*) And this one?

CROWD: (*Calling out together*) A cockroach!

SALESMAN: (*Showing yet another picture*) And this one?

CROWD: (*Calling out together*) A cockroach!

SALESMAN: You are right but, more precisely, these are pictures of drunken cockroaches. Now why are they drunk?

PERSON 1:   Too much booze!

(*The* CROWD *laughs.*)

SALESMAN: Because of insecticide, my friends. This is not magic. It's no spell. It's real. Buying an effective insecticide is different from buying an ineffective one, isn't that right?

CROWD: Right!

SALESMAN: Of course that's right. My friends, a cockroach is not a yam. A cockroach is not a staple food that can take the place of rice. Cockroaches are not shrimp they can't be eaten as food. On the other hand, cockroaches eat our food. That means that cockroaches are our enemy. One hundred percent enemies. So we have to wipe them out. So, let's go Indonesia! Together! One, two, one two...! (*Leading the crowd in song*)'

CROWD: *Flies, pests and roaches*
              We must wipe them out
              Flies, pests and roaches
              We must wipe them out

              Flies, pests and roaches
              The enemies of us all.
              Flies, pests and roaches
              The enemies of us all.

Do not let them breed and grow
Do not let them breed and grow.

Flies, pests and roaches
We must wipe them out
Flies, pests and roaches
The enemies of us all.

Do not let them breed and grow
Do not let them breed and grow.
Flies, pests and roaches! Yeah!

SALESMAN: (*Continuing his sales pitch*) Cockroaches are everywhere, ladies and gentlemen, throughout the enter world. Think about it. There are cockroaches in the United States, Yes, the U.S. of A. That very same country which is tops in so many fields—with good sanitation and effective democracy—still has cockroaches. I have read that in the United States for every one person there are 150 cockroaches. And what's the population of the United States? So how many cockroaches does that give you?

Now what about Indonesia? Don't even ask. With sanitation almost nonexistent and democracy ineffectual, for every one person there might well be 2000 cockroaches. Think about it: Let's say there are only 200 million people in this country. How many cockroaches does that make? Four hundred billion billion! God almighty, must we allow this to continue? No! It is our duty to wipe them out. It is everyone's duty.

That is why I am here: to help you. Vini, vidi, vici. I come, I sell, you buy. I am here to help you, with no pretense. I bring with me a cockroach spray.

(*People start to leave one by one.*)

PERSON 1:   I thought we'd get a freebie and here he gives us a lecture on cockroaches!

PERSON 2:   A damn salesman!

SALESMAN: Ladies, gentlemen, boys, girls, wait, wait!

PERSON 2:   Money's dear and better spent on rice than bug spray. Cockroaches?! We're used to cockroaches. Step into the gutter if you don't believe me.

SALESMAN: But I'm here to help. I'm not here to make a profit. My bug spray is cheap. I'd give it to you if I could. I'm an expert on cockroaches, an expert.

PERSON 1:   Ah, bullshit. Shut the fuck up! (*Throwing something at the* SALESMAN, *then exiting.*)

SALESMAN: (*Angrily and resentful*) Son-of-a-bitch, piss, fuck, bastard, cockroach!

(*People return to the places under the bridge.*)

LIGHTS CHANGE

7

Morning in the Jakarta slum. The sound of a fight erupts from one of the shacks and a RENT COLLECTOR *tumbles out of the doorway.* ASNAH, *an older woman from Sumatra appears at the door and begins to yell at the* RENT COLLECTOR. JULINI *and* ROMIA *watch the action.*

ASNAH: (*Speaking in Minangkabau*) I don't know. I already told you I don't know. Surti used to live here but I don't know where she is now. You're not going to try to get me to pay her debts. I'm not her mother or any relation at all.

RENT COLLECTOR: But she owes me! With interest I'm out one hundred thousand.

ASNAH: Out a million, that's your problem. I don't know where she is.

RENT COLLECTOR: If you don't have the money, then give me something of hers to pawn.

ASNAH: There's not a single thing of hers here. What do you want? Something of mine? Here, I'll give you something to pawn! (*Opens her sarong to expose herself*) Take it, it's yours!

RENT COLLECTOR: Watch it, lady. Next time I'm coming back with the police.

ASNAH: Fuck off. I've done nothing wrong. I'm not afraid of you.

RENT COLLECTOR: Up yours. I have a bodyguard you know.

ASNAH: Bodyguard, shit! All he can do is bark. The only thing big about him is him mouth. Show him my twat and he'd run away.

RENT COLLECTOR: So would I! Christ, you smell like an outhouse. And the only thing you got in there is cobwebs.

ASNAH: What's that you little shithead? You watch who you're talking to around here or I'll have your balls. Get out of here, now!

RENT COLLECTOR: (*Running away*) You just watch it. I'm warning you.

ASNAH: (*Grumbling as she goes back into the shack*) Damn greedy rent collector. Who does he think, he is? Probably hasn't had a good screw his whole life.

JULINI: (*Holding her nose*) My, my, isn't it odoriferous here? And my God, we haven't done anything and we're already caught in a war. Does Tuminah really live here?

ROIMA: I'm sure of it. Maybe not in one of the shacks but around here somewhere for sure.

JULINI:	Then what are we doing here?
ROIMA:	(*Looking around*) No harm in asking around, is there?
SALESMAN:	My fine friends, would you like to buy some cockroach spray? I have a large supply and cheap, too. Buy three, get one free! And effective. (*Imitates the sound of a spray can and a dead roach falling over*) Just psssss and plonk! And it lasts long, too.
JULINI:	Does it work on people?
SALESMAN:	(*Whispering*) Hey, who do you want to kill? A man or a woman? Age? Weight? Size?
JULINI:	Why all the questions?
SALESMAN:	Because all those factors influence its efficacy. Once you know them, we can figure the dosage for an instant K.O.
JULINI:	K.O.? You mean "dead?" (*Imitating a corpse*) Like that?
SALESMAN:	To put it bluntly, yes. Have you ever drunk poison?
JULINI:	Often. A love poison. Why?
SALESMAN:	You do a good imitation.
JULINI:	Basic talent is all.
SALESMAN:	How many bottles do you need? It's great as insecticide but it's also quite effective as a humanicide. That's efficiency for you. I'll give you a good price. A promotional price.
ROIMA:	(*Surprising* JULINI) Who do you want to poison?
JULINI:	You! No, no not you. I mean you startled me. You're always doing that.
ROIMA:	(*Pulling* JULINI's *arm*) Let's go.
SALESMAN:	Is it a sale or not?
JULINI:	Yeah, but later. Save one for me. (*Exits.*)

SALESMAN: Little drag queen. I bet she gets it everyday. Oh what a day, what a day.

LIGHTS CHANGE

8

Morning at the prostitution complex. The sun is bright. TARSIH *is leading the* PROSTITUTES *in an aerobics class. With a background of rock music, the* PROSTITUTES *are especially lively.* TUMINAH *is not to be seen.*

TARSIH: (*Addressing the* PROSTITUTES *in the manner and language of a government official giving a speech*) Ladies and gentlemen, it is a happy audience I have here today. As a developing nation and people, mental and physical rejuvenation is especially needed. The body and the soul. That is the reason for these morning exercises—for these too can be linked to the development of our people. Especially so in nurturing love for the cultural heritage of our own people. Also needed to nurture self-respect and self-awareness as important pillars of strength so that we can stand firmly as a free people who are healthy in both body and soul.

These movement are taken and developed from our own cultural resources. Thus it is logical these will help to nurture our love towards our own people and culture, which is an element for the growth of the our people in the future. (*Returning to her normal position and voice*) So that's it, that's how it is. That's why we have to exercise...

PROSTITUTES: Yes, Ma'am!

TARSIH: Exercise is important, especially for those of us who have to work hard day and night and be ready to belly dance at a moment's notice. Exercise tightens those muscles.... Which is very important for the satisfaction of our customers. If our customers are happy, the money is there for the taking. But if they're not satisfied, all we get is a kick in the butt. Music!

(*Aerobics music erupts from* BODIGAR*'s cassette player.*)

ALL: And one and two and three and four... (*Repeating.*)

TARSIH: And one and two and three and four.... Repeat and then try it on your own. Yeah!

(*The* PROSTITUTES's *start doing their own moves.* TUMINAH *comes out of the second floor of the whore house. She has with her a customer, the* HIGH OFFICIAL. *They look to be especially intimate.*)

TUMINAH: Will I see you again, sir?

HIGH OFFICIAL: I told you not to call me "sir"?

TUMINAH: I'm sorry. When will you come again, sweetheart?

HIGH OFFICIAL: Again and again, Tuminah. You are special, Tuminah. Incredible. You never fail to satisfy. You're different from the others.

TUMINAH: What do you mean "different?"

HIGH OFFICIAL: I don't know, just different; always ready to show me something new. For me, it's always a special experience with you.

TUMINAH: Why? Because at home you can't, uh, try something new?

HIGH OFFICIAL: At home monotony rules: the same position for thirty years. My wife doesn't like anything strange. Off goes the light, she opens her robe, rub-a-dub-dub, three minutes later it's over and she starts to snore. There's no sweet talk. She doesn't like it; she thinks it's juvenile.

TUMINAH: Then get yourself another one.

HIGH OFFICIAL: Another wife? I'd lose my job. People in my position aren't supposed to have two wives. The people upstairs don't like it. Play around if you want, but take another wife? Hold on. The VIP Wives Club is very influential. And the more power they get the more arbitrary with power they are. Meanwhile we, the husbands, can only scratch our heads. But anyway, enough said, I have to go home.

TUMINAH: First give me a kiss.

HIGH OFFICIAL: (*Kissing* TUMINAH) Mmm, so sweet. Just like honey. Bye...

TUMINAH: Bye.

(*On the last step of the flight of stairs, the* HIGH OFFICIAL *catches his foot in a hole and takes a tumble.*)

HIGH OFFICIAL: Owww!

TUMINAH: Be careful: there are lots of holes around here.

HIGH OFFICIAL: (*Spoken from amidst the* PROSTITUTES*'s who are exercising*) There sure are! It was my fault. I wasn't concentrating. You are something. Bye. (*Quickly exiting.*)

TARSIH: (*Still leading exercises*) And one and two and three and four. Shake out those muscles, Sri. Stick out your boobs out, Ade. And Rita, don't hold your breath. Let it all out. While moaning if you must. That's important too. Come on, moan.... (*Moaning*) Breathe while moaning...

(*All of the* PROSTITUTES*'s follow suit.*)

That's good. Go on. (*To* TUMINAH) If you're finished, Tuminah, join in.

TUMINAH: I still have five more clients.

TARSIH:	Tell them to wait; they won't go anywhere.
TUMINAH:	Alright. (*She rips off her outer clothing to reveal an aerobics outfit.*)

(ROIMA *and* JULINI *enter.*)

JULINI:	(*Happily*) Look, it's Tuminah. I wonder if she'll recognize me? But she's busy. Let's wait to catch her after she's finished her tai-chi. She gets better looking all the time. And there's Tarsih! It's just like a reunion.

(JULINI *starts to exercise too but in a most uncoordinated fashion and keeps falling then picking herself up.* ROIMA *watches.*)

TUMINAH:	(*Seeing* JULINI) Julini? Is that you, Julini? Tarsih, it's Julini. (*Running to* JULINI) Oh, you're still alive!
JULINI:	Still surviving is more like it.
TARSIH:	(*In a cold unfriendly voice*) Oh, Julini. How are you?

(*The class stops its exercise.*)

TUMINAH:	How did you know I was here?
JULINI:	Where's the paper, hon? Here it is. I saw your photo in the paper. Look, there's even a circle around your head! It's good they didn't blacken out your eyes.
TUMINAH:	Oh, that was one of those "Who's in the Picture" contests. But that was seven months ago.
JULINI:	But it gives your address. And it says you got a gas stove. Talk about modern; a gas stove and everything!
TARSIH:	(*To the* PROSTITUTES*'s*) Okay, girls, class is over.

(*The* PROSTITUTES *leave.*)

JULINI:	You look like you're doing all right, Tarsih.

TARSIH:	Not, bad. But this kind of business is good anywhere, especially with the number of frustrated husbands there are nowadays. Just read the papers if you want to check on the divorce rate.
JULINI:	I know, I know. But we'll never get divorced. I'll always be there for my Roima, unless a bullet gets me first.
ROIMA:	Knock on wood!
TARSIH:	So, what are you doing here, Julini?
TUMINAH:	How about we wait till later with your questions? Julini must be tired. Have you two eaten?
TARSIH:	No. Tuminah. Jumini might be an old friend but it's best to find out what exactly she's doing here.

We've had experience with old friends before, remember? I'm not going to be taken advantage of again. Think of what happened to you; how you gave your honor to that pack of assholes. All for your brother!

And the result? You lost everything anyway and your brother went to jail. You have to be hard, Tum. You have to, that's if you have any concern for yourself. Help people, fine, but you should get something in return. That's how you get by in the big city. If you're weak, you're dead.

TUMINAH:	What are you talking about? Julini just got here and you're already suspicious. Just because she's from the village doesn't mean...
TARSIH:	People know that we're successful. So when they come here, it's usually because they're looking for help.
TUMINAH:	Well, if we're in a position to help, we should.
TARSIH:	And what good does that bring you?
TUMINAH:	They're our friends, aren't they.

JULINI: Don't get into an argument over me. I came here because I missed you; that's all. Really, I missed you is all. Why should we want your help? Roima here has a job in a cable factory. I just wanted to let you know that we're back.

ROIMA: (*Impatient*) Come on, let's go!

(ROIMA *and* JULINI *leave.* TUMINAH *watches.* TARSIH *shrugs her shoulders.*)

TUMINAH: Wait. Where are you going.

JULINI: (*Confused*) To the cable factory, I suppose...

ROIMA: (*Dragging* JULINI *away*) Come on and do what I say. Let's go.

(*They exit.* TUMINAH *stands in silence.* TARSIH *looks like she's feeling guilty.*)

TARSIH: (*Defensively*) Well, I didn't mean to chase them away.

TUMINAH: The big city turns people into sadists.

(TUMINAH *goes inside.* TARSIH *stands silents, alone and confused.*)

LIGHTS CHANGE

9

A golf course. ROIMA *and* JULINI *rest on the green. While* JULINI *seems bewildered,* ROIMA *is angry.*

ROIMA: That no-good good-for-nothing little slut...!

JULINI: How could she have changed? You remember how nice Tarsih used to be?

ROIMA: And you saying that I work in a cable factory. A cable factory? Why didn't you say that we're looking for work. What's the big deal?

JULINI: Don't be that way, hon. I've known you a long time. You're proud and if I had asked for help, you would have gotten angry. Maybe we do need help but we shouldn't have to beg for it. If they want to help us, they will.

ROIMA: I've changed, you know, changed a lot.

JULINI: So now you tell me! Why didn't you give me a little time so that I could be prepared. It's always like that. You never tell me anything until it's too late. Now what are we supposed to do? Go back to the village?

ROIMA: "Back to the village...." It sounds like the title of a goddamned film. Son of a bitch! I'll show her. For now we'll just have to try to make it on our own.

JULINI: (*Sighing*) Well, I could turn some tricks for a while.

ROIMA: To survive, we have to be able to do anything.

(*A whistle blows. The sound grows louder.*)

JULINI: Lord, we can't get away from them. They're all over the place. What is this place anyway? So wide and green... must be a playing field.

(*A SECURITY GUARD enters.*)

SECURITY GUARD 1: It's a golf course, idiot. Now get out of here!

JULINI: Where are we supposed to go? No one will have us. It's like we're strangers in a strange land even though we have identity cards.

SECURITY GUARD 1: Don't make trouble. Move on. There are important people around here.

(*In the slum area, people stick their heads out from the gutters at the sound of a siren. The prostitutes stick their heads out of their windows. Everyone looks in the direction of the golf course, staring as if they are watching an outdoor film.)*

PERSON 1:   Hey, hey, over here.

ASNAH: Don't stand there. You could get shot.

(JULINI *and* ROIMA *join the* SLUM DWELLERS.)

JULINI: What is going on? Is it war?

ASNAH: No, but the same thing: golf.

PERSON 2:   Here we have the high government official on the one side playing with a foreign visitor on the other while they talk about the fate of the common people.

PERSON 1:   Shhh, they're coming.

(The BODYGUARDS *and* MEDIA PEOPLE *enter. One of the reporters starts taking photographs. When the* HIGH OFFICIAL *and a* FOREIGN VISITOR [VISITOR] *enter, the* MEDIA PEOPLE *go into a flurry of activity. Camera lights flash. The* HIGH OFFICIAL *and the* VISITOR *are dressed in sports clothing. Each is carrying a golf club; each has a* CADDY *behind him. The* SLUM DWELLERS *are enjoying the show.)*

HIGH OFFICIAL: My friendship with your people, sir, has reached a promising level. The attention of the entire world is on us now. Your offer of soft-term loans is truly generous. Have faith that the funds you contribute will be put toward the betterment of our people. And that they will certainly be very grateful.

VISITOR: *(Spoken with a heavy Japanese accent)* Of course, of course. Assistance to the developing countries is our major priority. We have money; your people have ideals, and it is our duty to help you achieve your ideals. What is it...? *(Taking a piece of paper from his pocket)* "To utilize credit for the prosperity of the people. Development shall focus on only those activities which are of direct benefit to the people. Projects that are considered wasteful or redundant shall be reviewed and replaced with multipurpose project. As such, this assistance cannot be seen from a financial point of view only. It represents a human effort to help our fellows as brothers of Mankind." (*Everyone claps*) Bravo, I say. This article is very interesting.

HIGH OFFICIAL: The important thing is that credit is released quickly. We're have pressing needs.

VISITOR: Of course, of course. But one for me, one for you. Five percent each, is that alright?

HIGH OFFICIAL: There's no need to discuss that. What's important is that we are working together for the prosperity of our countries. The question of personal profit has no relevance.... But the five percent could be transferred directly to my Swiss bank account: Number... (*Shows the* VISITOR *his bank account number.*)

VISITOR: Fine, fine, (*Everyone claps*) As a formality, however, please allow me to visit those areas that you deem to be developmental success stories.

HIGH OFFICIAL: Oh, yes, of course, that can be arranged.

(*The* HIGH OFFICIAL *calls an* UNDERLING *and whispers something to him. The latter then goes to where the* MEDIA PEOPLE *are standing.*)

UNDERLING: Ladies and gentlemen, the official part of the ceremony is now over. Our esteemed government official and our honored visitor would now like to continue with a program of a more private nature. Please excuse us for now. You will get a written press release by this evening and, of course, a little something extra as a sign of our appreciation for your hard work.

(*The* MEDIA PEOPLE *leave without protest. The* HIGH OFFICIAL *and the* VISITOR *sit on a tatami mat and drink sake.*)

HIGH OFFICIAL: Now it's time to relax. With all the work we do for our people, we should be granted moment of pleasure for ourselves.

VISITOR: Of course; I quite agree.

HIGH OFFICIAL: I imagine that in your country there are numerous and pleasant places to relax.

VISITOR: Yes, there are.

HIGH OFFICIAL: And ladies?

VISITOR: Yes, and ladies, too.

HIGH OFFICIAL: And do you often make use of such pleasures? Karaoke, geishas...?

VISITOR: Well, sometimes.... (*Whispering*) But I'm sure the ladies of your country are no less entertaining. I've heard tales about the gentle arts of island girls.

HIGH OFFICIAL: (*Laughing*) Well if you are up to it, I can take you to a place I know. Would you like that?

VISITOR: I'd like that very much.

(*The* PROSTITUTES *who have been watching the scene from* TARSIH's *place begin to whistle and clap their hands.*)

HIGH OFFICIAL: Now?

VISITOR: Now.

(*They proceed to* TARSIH's *place, singing "Nona Manis Siapa*

Yang Punya" as they go. Both are somewhat inebriated. When they arrive at the bordello, the HIGH OFFICIAL *knocks on the door.)*

HIGH OFFICIAL: (*Loudly*) Tuminah, honey, I've brought a guest with me!

(*They enter.*)

LIGHTS CHANGE

10

Morning. At the SLUM DWELLERS' *shacks. Now that the "show" is over, everyone has returned to their daily chores.*

ASNAH: Are you just in from the village?

JULINI: Yeah, but we used to live here, that is, till we got evicted. But now we're back again. I mean, what was I supposed to do in the village? I don't know how to use a shovel and there's no demand for a masseuse. I tried opening a little stall—to sell things, you know—but that went belly up. It was all IOUs. So we packed up and...

ALI.: (*Singing*) *And so back to Jakarta, I came...*

JULINI: How'd you guess?

ASNAH: So where are you staying?

JULINI: I don't know yet.

ASNAH: Well, if you want, there' s bit of unused space here. It's only a couple square meters but it should do. And it's my stake, so if you want to stay there, just tell me.

JULINI: How about it, Roima?

ROIMA: You take care of it. I've got some things I want to do. I've got to go. See you later (*He hurries away.*)

ASNAH: Is that your boyfriend? Looks like he'd bite your head off.

JULINI: He gets like that sometimes, but he has a good heart. Used to be, he always had to have his way, but now he gives in most of the time. In bed, he always used to be on top but now, every once in a while, he takes the bottom, too. It's kind of like a wheel, I suppose. Sometimes up, sometimes down, all depends on what turns you on. By the way, what's your name?

ASNAH: Asnah.

JULINI: Might you tell me, is there any demand for a masseuse around here?

ASNAH: If all you can do is massage, forget it. But if you're a "masseuse-plus," it's the extra stuff that sells.

JULINI: Well, that's what I meant. I used to be "masseuse plus" and, I tell you, I felt like I was a bank teller with my customers coming back for more and more deposits. I was good at it, that's why. But now, being out of the business for so long, all my customers have probably gone.

ASNAH: You'll have to start from the bottom again.

(From one of the huts comes the sound of a woman singing. Her off-pitch song is interspersed with laughter and weeping.)

JULINI: What's that?

ASNAH: That one? She used to be a whore. Was quite the thing but now she's old and eaten away by syphilis. She's lost her mind...

JULINI: Poor thing.

KASIJAH: *(Singing) We are yams, we are rice*
Ye are cattle, we are swine.
We are dreams, we are shit

Oh me, oh God, the pain. It's all gone, everything's all gone! God in heaven, why do you punish me so? Let me die. Let me die...

JULINI: Her voice sounds familiar. Who is it?

ASNAH: Kasijah.

JULINI: Oh my God! Kasijah? I know her! Is that where she lives?

(JULINI *goes to* KASIJAH's *shack.*)

ASNAH: Yeah.

JULINI: (*Looking inside*) Kasijah?

KASIJAH: (*Continuing to wail*) Wowowowo, wiwiwiwi...

ASNAH: She's lost one nut too many. Forget it. She won't remember. All she can think about is pain.

JULINI: Oh, the poor thing. A comrade in the struggle, she was. And now look at what's happened. (*Poetically, with tears in her eyes*) Trying to forget your suffering is like trying to rid yourself of your own shadow. (*Everyone claps*) Oh, gosh, I'm really sad.

PERSON 1:   So true...

11

Night. At the prostitution complex. Afternoon. The PROSTITUTES *are relaxing and singing "A Handful of Flowers." As they are doing this,* ROIMA *sneaks into* TUMINAH's *room but then a short while later exits.*)

PROSTITUTES: *A handful of flowers so fragrant their scent*
             Playing with the wind, yes the wind
             Facing the sun, the bright light
             The bright light, my sweet, bright light

A handful of flowers, bitter is their fate
When fragrant, sought by the bees
But wilted, are thrown away
Thrown away, my sweet, thrown away

We are a handful of flowers
Your love was for a moment only
With sweet talk alone you had your way
But once satisfied, kicked me aside

Oh, just a handful of flowers
Oh, just a handful of flowers

TUMINAH: (*Coming out from her room and joining the* PROSTITUTES) And so knowing that we will be kicked aside, it makes sense for us to make money where we can. We need as much as possible.

PROSTITUTE 1: For the future.

PROSTITUTE 2: And when we have enough money we'll go to Singapore. A nip here, a tuck there and we come back as virgins! Then we'll go back home and marry the village big cheese.

PROSTITUTE 3: If the in-laws ask you what you did in Jakarta, answer demurely, "Oh, a little business."

PROSTITUTE 4: "Marketing."

PROSTITUTE 5: "The private sector."

TUMINAH: (*As if giving a speech*) But believe me, my friends, we know that we must return to the righteous path, that this path of vice is only temporary. (*They laugh uproariously.*)

(TARSIH *enters.*)

PROSTITUTE 4: Shhh...

TARSIH: I got some news for you. Here, look at this flyer I received.

TUMINAH: What's it about?

TARSIH: Income taxes.

PROSTITUTE 2: Taxes?

TARSIH: Well it does make sense. After all, I mean, businesses are taxed everywhere. We should be proud that from our hard work we are able to contribute to the benefit of this country. According to this, we are to be charged a personal income tax of 17%, a Value Added Tax of 10%, an entertainment tax of 20% and a business tax of 25% calculated from the general rate.

              And that there will be strict supervision to limit room for fraud. Tax fraud's a criminal offense. You can be put in jail. So what we're going to have to do is to raise our rates. By what...? 17 plus 10 plus 20 plus 25 is 72%. There's no way but to off-load the tax burden onto the customer.

              (*The* PROSTITUTES *grumble and mutter.*)

TUMINAH: But won't they protest?

TARSIH: Not if they're desperate. Remember, the men who come here are desperate. And your task is to make them more desperate.

PROSTITUTE 4: But if they're desperate and broke?

TARSIH: Turn them away. We will only accept, *must* only accept, those with money.

PROSTITUTE 2: But what about our boyfriends?

TARSIH: (*Angrily*) Especially them! Forget them! Now's the time to gather resources, not to take care of boyfriends—that's if you have any concern for yourself at all. Nobody else is going to take care of you. We have to watch what we spend and not let ourselves be swindled. And boyfriends, more often than not, are swindlers. If we were men, it wouldn't be a big deal. But we're women. And once deceived, our future is lost. Who is it who deceives? It's men, that's who, our boyfriends. (*She stomps angrily into her room.*)

TUMINAH: Her boyfriends were always taking advantage of her.

PROSTITUTE 2: Even so, she shouldn't generalize.

(*All the* PROSTITUTES *return to their rooms.*)

LIGHTS CHANGE

12

Afternoon. At the intersection near the slum. The SALESMAN *has laid out his wares and is beating a tambourine to attract attention.*

SALESMAN: Believe me, ladies and gentlemen, I'm not crazy. The situation is serious and that's why I am serious, too. The threat of cockroaches is growing. Through the centuries countless attempts have been made to exterminate them. And over time they have built up a kind of antitoxin, thereby making the offspring of the ancestral cockroaches even more immune. A regular spray won't help; it's useless! Today's cockroaches are wearing helmets and safety belts. That's why I present this superior spray. Try it. Danger is on its way. Cockroaches! Why this spray's so good you can use it on people too. If you don't believe me, just try, at your own risk of course.

(*Someone from the slum throws a stone at the* SALESMAN. *Others follows suit. The* SALESMAN *tries to keep from being hit.*)

Hey, stop that! What did I do? Help! Help!

(*He hurriedly gathers his things and exits.*)

LIGHTS CHANGE

13

Night. Gang headquarters. KUMIS, *the local gang leader, is meeting with* BLEKI, *his assistant, and other* GANG MEMBERS *who attentively listen to him as he speaks.* ROIMA *and* TUMINAH *are also in the crowd. Both* KUMIS *and* BLEKI *laugh as the scene begins.*

KUMIS: I bet you're surprised to see me. I used to be head of the local watchmen; now I'm head of the mob. (*Laughing.*)

(BLEKI *laughs too.*)

But those days are over. Now is the age of "security." The job's the same all right, but the perception is different. As a local watchman, all you got was a pair of used army boots. But a security guard gets handcuffs and a billy club, sometimes even torture equipment. (*Laughing.*)

(BLEKI *laughs again.*)

Shut your mouth, shit-for-brains.

(BLEKI *looks frightened.*)

They fired me as a watchman because they didn't think I could do the job. So what was I supposed to do? Apply for a job as a security guard? Too much competition. Besides, I can't read or write.

If you don't have a job, life in Jakarta is tough. You're a worm to be stomped on. What am I going to do? Beg? That's a sin. What am I supposed to do with these muscles of mine? I'll tell ya: as a watchman, I got to know the holes for opportunity.

BLEKI: And then...!

KUMIS: (*Slapping* BLEKI) Shut up, you fool. I'm not finished talking. Five years as my assistant and your brain is still in your belly button. Dumb shit.

TUMINAH: So is Roima in or not?

BLEKI: Sure, sure.... (*Scooting away before* KUMIS *can slap him again*) Sorry, boss, sorry. I can't get my mouth to shut up. (*Slapping himself time and again.*) Shut the fuck up, shut the fuck up.

KUMIS: Well, Roima, you've come to the right place, and at the right time, too. I have lots of guys applying for work but I'm forced to turn them away. Being a bandit these days ain't easy; you have to be screened first. Quality's the key word. We put a high price on quality. And our screening process is stricter that it is for the civil service.

TUMINAH: So is he in or not?

BLEKI: Of course, he's in.... (*Running away again*) Sorry, boss, sorry. Just can't help myself.

TUMINAH: So, Kumis, is he in?

KUMIS: Yeah, he's in.

TUMINAH: Thanks, Kumis. And no catches, right?

KUMIS: You're a smart woman, Tuminah. My sweet talk gets nowhere with you. But I do remember when I had you that first time. Hmm, that was special; and not something I'll forget. Yup, pure pleasure was the word.

TUMINAH: You can still sleep with me, as long as you pay the right price. I'm everybody's girl now.

KUMIS: And that's what I won't have. I want love. Whoever said a bandit doesn't want love? Love, Tuminah, love.

TUMINAH: (*Laughing*) Well I have to get going, Kumis. Tarsih will be looking for me. I'll leave Roima with you. Give him some pointers. (*Exits.*)

KUMIS: She's something. Her body, her movement, her passion…

BLEKI: (*To* ROIMA) Is she your girlfriend?

ROIMA: No, you know Julini's my girlfriend.

BLEKI: So? What's wrong with a little switch hit?

KUMIS: Okay boys, we've got a new buddy. And, like usual, he has to be initiated. Give me the tool, Bleki.

BLEKI: Sure, boss. (*Getting a cudgel.*)

KUMIS: Bend over!

(BLEKI *bends over.*)

Not you, idiot. Roima!

(ROIMA *bends over and one by one, the* GANG MEMBERS *paddle his backside and then urinate on him.* KUMIS *is the last.*)

KUMIS: Now we have to be faithful and loyal. There must be no treachery. And if you're caught by the police, you're on your own. No bringing in friends' names. Agreed?

ROIMA: Agreed!

KUMIS: Now let's recite our oath of loyalty.

(*All sing "Wild Dogs"*)

ALL: *We are wild dogs*
Shit and gold's our food.
We can't live off pity

Happiness must be stolen
With our minds, with our hands

With force
Or in misery we'll remain.

We are wild dogs
Ready to fight if need be.
Money doesn't fall from the sky
And prayer is often useless.
Where is there honor?
It comes from power and wealth!
Embrace them, embrace them

Or downtrodden we'll remain
Or downtrodden we'll remain.

LIGHTS CHANGE

14

Night. The prostitution complex. Outside TUMINAH's *room is a row of customers. Clients come and go. The atmosphere is festive, like that of a night fair but* TARSIH *is seated alone in thought in her room. When* JULINI *appears, she is greeted enthusiastically by the* PROSTITUTES.

PROSTITUTE 1: Julini! Julini!

PROSTITUTE 2: Are you peddling here, Jul?

JULINI: Here? Now way. I have my own place. The johns who come here are looking for girls, not a tranny. If it's a kick in the ass I want, I can get that elsewhere. Here, I brought you something. A cake.

PROSTITUTE 3: What's in it? Poison?

JULINI: That's right. Eat it and croak.

PROSTITUTE 1: You look great, Julini, so up-to-date with that red wig of yours. Just like a swinging single! Or a punk rocker, maybe. Trying to be fashionable, eh?

JULINI: Call me what you will: a swinging single, a punk rocker or a punk wheelchair, for that matter; what's important for me is business. And services! If a customer wants something a little odd, that's what I give him. If he wants traditional, I put on my batik sarong and high heels. Blisters, never mind, if that's what my customer wants.

PROSTITUTE 4: Getting busy, huh?

JULINI: Compared to the number of Johns around here, at my place they're queued up.

PROSTITUTE 1: Well if you're so busy, what are you doing here? It's only 11 o'clock.

JULINI: Restless is all. Between 8 and 10, I had ten customers. Think of how long that is for each one. Just ten minutes! Think of how desperate they must be. Why, they haven't even gotten their pants down before, oops, thar she blows! Some don't even get that far. I had this one guy with this whopper of a moustache and, oooh, did he look mean. But once we got in the room, all he could do was stare.

PROSTITUTE 5: Stare?

JULINI: Yeah, no kidding; all he did was stare. And then he started to sweat. His shirt, his jeans were wringing wet, like he'd been dunked in a pool. He shook and stared and growled and then started at me again. Then, all of a sudden, he slumped in the chair.

PROSTITUTE 1: Then what happened?

JULINI: Nothing. He paid me. And he hadn't even done anything. Crazy, huh? These days, it seems that more and more men only like to do it with men. Weird...

PROSTITUTE 2: You're joking.

JULINI: No, it's true. They themselves have told me so. I ask them, why don't you go to Tarsih's place? There's lots of pretty girls over there. And they tell me they're bored with women. Bored! And I say, what's the difference? It's all the same, isn't it? And they get mad and say it's not the same. If it were the same, one guy said, an exhaust pipe would do.

(*The* PROSTITUTES *laugh.*)

Sorry, this kind of talk is for married ladies only. So all you virgin girls out there, shut your ears. This is sex education, honey. Anyway, I mean, well, on the outside we're all laughing, but on the inside it's heartbreak hotel. I'm serious. We're not doing this because we want to. We're forced to. So if you can be a secretary, be one. You'll be much better off.

The heart wants to hug a mountain, but what can you do with a broken wrist...?

PROSTITUTE 1: But doesn't Roima get jealous?

JULINI: Jealous? Shit. He's the one who suggested it. How else are we supposed to eat? You can't eat jealousy. It's just hot air, and the only thing you get from that is farts. Besides, this is a business, just like any other. Good or bad, we're responsible for ourselves. People like to pooh pooh and wag their tongues, but try asking them for a job or a little handout and see where their mouths are at. You can't even get your foot in the gate. They all have big signs, "Beware of Dogs." It's all fine and good for them to ask, "Why don't you look for a decent job?" We can look, sure, but doing what? Why should we be the butt of their jokes? This is our bowl of rice. This is work; that's what it is.

PROSTITUTE 4: But you're doing well, aren't you, Jul?

JULINI: Not bad. Good enough anyway to buy me some imported bras and undies. Customers like cleanliness, you know, and colored undies turn them on. You should see the new ones I got. They're real cute, with embroidered roses...

(The PROSTITUTES *pinch* JULINI *and they laugh.* JULINI *then starts to sings the song "The Three Pleasures."* The PROSTITUTES *follow along stutteringly.* TUMINAH *is with* TARSIH.)

What is it they're looking for?
The three pleasures, my love, three pleasures
The you-know-what, the mouth and the mind
All three are very necessary.

But to have them, my love
The three pleasures, the three pleasures
You need to pay, you need money
There's nothing in this world for free.

What can be sold, we sell
We will do anything to live
Fate is in our own hands
Who else cares about us, who else?

Oh, when I think about it, I could go on and on. Look at what life has dished out to us and all those other people can do is criticize. (*She starts to run away.*)

TUMINAH: Jul, where are you going, Jul?

JULINI: Home! Roima will be mad if I'm late

(JULINI *begins to run away but trip and falls. She screams out and the* PROSTITUTES *repeat her cry. She rises, calls out good-bye and then exits. The* PROSTITUTES *go on with what they were doing.*)

TARSIH: Julini might be a flibbertigibbet but she's right. I'm glad she doesn't hold a grudge against me. We are the wretched. People think our work is disgusting but do they think we want to forever live in the gutter? No way.

TUMINAH: You're right.

(*One of the* PROSTITUTES *sings "The Song of Impropriety" in a slow voice.*)

PROSTITUTE: *Happy, my love, I'm happy*
In a life of sin and filth
Wishing for, but finding naught
What's the meaning of joy?

The earth and sky revile us
Our world is completely dark
Light is only a dream
Only a dream, my love, a dream.

We are only moths
Flying about, flapping our wings
Happy for a moment only
Then dying, consumed by the flame.

My song is one of impropriety
A song of the discarded
A song of the hopeless
A song of the owl that pines for the moon.

My song is one of impropriety
Impropriety, my love, impropriety.

(TARSIH *begins to cry.*)

TUMINAH: Oh, don't do that Tarsih. We all need people like you. I don't know what would have happened to me if hadn't met you. With both my parents dead and my only brother in jail, what was a fool like me supposed to do?

TARSIH: Do you really think I'm of any use?

TUMINAH: Of course you are. And if we support each other we'll be strong. People feel weak then they feel alone.

TARSIH: Thank you, Tuminah, thank you.

LIGHTS CHANGE

15

Morning. A development project site. A large billboard shows plans for the site but, at present, it is still a slum. Financing for this site, which has come from foreign creditors, is intended to become an elite location. SECURITY GUARDS *are covering the shacks with white sheeting prior to the arrival of the* HIGH OFFICIAL *and* FOREIGN VISITOR.

VISITOR: (*Chit-chat*) Wonderful. Great. Satisfied. A case of foreign aid that has been utilized appropriately. I will report on all of this.

HIGH OFFICIAL: This is nothing yet. On that empty area of land over there we're going to build schools, libraries, place of worship and markets for small traders. This is the realization of the economic principles that we follow, that being that everything necessary for the betterment of the people, for equitable distribution of the cake/results of development.

VISITOR: A noble plan indeed; amazing. We have no regrets at all about assisting you in the realization of this noble plan. None at all. This is truly wonderful. (*Clicking his tongue.*)

HIGH OFFICIAL: And not only that—we are paying attention to art and culture as well. We will erect facilities for all of that over there. Yes, over there.

To ensure the continued vitality of the arts, both modern and traditional, we will continue to subsidize them. This is important, and of course this has been the nature of our people since the age of Majapahit and the Javanese kings. Research projects on traditional culture are top priority. Ancient remains are to be rebuilt, all of them, and even cemeteries revered by their communities will be restored.

Our descendants must know that we were people with respect for ancestral history; yes, a generation with respect for cemeteries.

VISITOR: That's true, true. Once again, extraordinary. Restoring all cemeteries, eh? All cemeteries...

HIGH OFFICIAL: (*With pride*) And museums, too. We'll build them everywhere. This is important, because only an ignorant people would care nothing about documenting the history of the past. And monuments. We will erect a monument for each event, the common ones as well as the heroic. If there are a million heroes, we'll build a million monuments.

We'll take note immediately of everything that touches the heart of the community. Yes, we'll build a monument.

Those who belong to the Grouch and Grumble Brigade say that rice is more important than monuments. But we and the masses say: Monuments are important. Monuments are like a pair of trousers. Civilization.

VISITOR: Great! Once more, amazing. With this, I can go home to my country with enormous satisfaction. Wonderful. Thank you.

HIGH OFFICIAL: Is there anything else you'd like to see, sir?

VISITOR: Enough, enough. What I see here gives me the total picture. My task is finished and... (*Whispering*) let's go back to your girlfriend. What's her name?

HIGH OFFICIAL: (*Whispering*) Tuminah.

VISITOR: She too was wonderful. Just like this project. Shall we go now?

HIGH OFFICIAL: Now?

VISITOR: Yes, now.

VISITOR: Alright then, let's go.

(*They exit, while singing "Nona Manis." As soon as they leave, the* SECURITY GUARDS *remove the white sheeting from the shacks and take down the sign. Inside their huts the* SLUM DWELLERS *can only watch. The* SECURITY GUARDS *exit.*)

LIGHTS CHANGE

16

Evening. Beneath a bridge in the slum. ROIMA *and* TUMINAH *enter followed by the* SALESMAN *and then* JULINI.

SALESMAN: (*Only passing by*) Bug spray, cockroach spray. Get the job done right! Buy three get a fourth one free. Bug spray, anti-bug spray!

ROIMA: And so?

TUMINAH: I'm afraid. He'll be mad for sure. He thinks I'm a respectable woman. He doesn't know that I...

ROIMA: Tibal has to understand. He shouldn't be that way. You're just a victim of circumstance.

TUMINAH: But when Tibal gets mad he loses control. He's very hard headed. If he finds out what I'm doing now, he'll kill me for sure. I'm afraid.

ROIMA:	That was Tibal's fault. Why did he go crazy and kill that official? He was irresponsible; he didn't think about you at all.
TUMINAH:	But now he's out and he's sure to have it in for Kumis. What am I supposed to do?
ROIMA:	Let me talk to him. If anything happens, I'll protect you.
TUMINAH:	(*Taking his hand*) Roima...
ROIMA:	(*Taking her hand and sighing*) I have to go... Julini will be waiting for me at home.
TUMINAH:	I know, you're Julini's man. I keep forgetting.
JULINI:	(*From offstage*) Roima, Roima, Roiiimmmaa...!
ROIMA:	I have to go. We'll see each other later. (*Exits quickly.*)
	(TUMINAH *stares blankly.* JULINI *enters.*)
JULINI:	Tuminah. Have you see Roima?
TUMINAH:	(*Shaking her head*) Nope.
JULINI:	Where is he? He promised to be home early. And I cooked his favorite dish! It's getting dark and I have to get to work....We don't see each other much these days. When I get home, he's not there. He always says Kumis has work for him to do. He tells me too that he's been finding out lots of ways of making extra on the side. Is that true?
TUMINAH:	How should I know, Jul?
JULINI:	Just thought you might have heard something.
TUMINAH:	Nah, haven't heard a thing.
JULINI:	What, are you deaf or something? But it's true, there are lots of ways of making money. Rich people don't seem to know what to do with their money nowadays. They have their larks. They come out with their hard-ons and where

do they look for ass? Along the river banks and the gutter! I ask them why not go to a hotel? Experience, they tell me, they want the experience. Well, if they get AIDS or something, then they'll know what experience is.

TUMINAH: Those are nice clothes you're wearing.

JULINI: Gifts from heaven! God is good and Roima's bringing home money, too. It's not like before looking for handouts. Now we're putting money aside and when we have enough we're going to open a salon. Not, here, though, farther out.

TUMINAH: Don't you want to get married, Jul?

JULINI: Married? We once wanted to but it didn't work out. So we started to think what is the use of a marriage certificate anyway. I mean, why not cohabilate?

TUMINAH: Cohabitate.

JULINI: Yeah, whatever. And because we're not a man and a woman, nobody is going to bother us. It would be different if you, let's say, were to cobiltitate with Roima.

TUMINAH: It's "cohabitate."

JULINI: Yeah, yeah, whatever it is. What's the difference? The important part is the "co," right? Anyway, this way I feel so modern. It's like being a film star. But, sometimes, it's sad, too. I'd like to have a child but I can't. And an operation would cost the sky. I get so down sometimes. But did you see Roima or not?

(TUMINAH *shakes her head.*)

Well then, I'll have to go look for him. Roima.... Roima! Where are you? Let's not play hide and seek. (*She exits.*)

TUMINAH: (*Irritated with herself*) Shit! (*Exits.*)

LIGHTS CHANGE

17

Night. Gang headquarters. KUMIS, seated like a king, is surrounded by BLEKI, ROIMA and other gang members. BLEKI massages KUMIS's shoulders as GANGSTERS report to him.

KUMIS: (*With his eyes closed*) The representative from Blok-M area.

GANGSTER 1: Present. Everything's fine, boss. My deposit is commensurate with the request.

KUMIS: It should be larger; your area's the busiest. Next month add 20% to the deposit.

GANGSTER 1: Yes, boss

KUMIS: The representative from Glodok, Hayam Wuruk, Gajah Mada and Roxi.

GANGSTER 2: Sorry to say, Boss, but business is down. You got places either closed or burnt out. But I have a gift for you, too. It's antique, boss, carved ivory. (*Handing KUMIS the cane*) See for yourself.

KUMIS: Thank you. But if you're going to make jokes, then learn to make them at the proper time. Are you trying to say that I'm too old, that maybe I should retire? Whether this cane is gold or ivory, I don't care. A slight is still a slight. Beat him up, Roima.

ROIMA: Sure, boss. (*To GANGSTER 2.*) Bend over.

(ROIMA *beats* GANGSTER 2 *with the cane.*)

GANGSTER 2: (*After being beaten*) Thank you, boss.

KUMIS: No more jokes from here on; you got it.

GANGSTER 2: Got it, boss.

KUMIS: And the rest of you, put your deposit in a pile behind Bleki and then get out of here. I got nothing new to tell you; just that everything is okay.

(*As the* GANGSTERS *begin leave,* KUMIS *remembers something.*)

Hey, wait a minute. Where's the representative from Airport Toll Road?

(*The* GANGSTERS *gather again.*)

GANGSTER 3: Here, Boss.

KUMIS: What's the situation like out there?

GANGSTER 3: Getting busier all the time, Boss. The pickings are good both day and night. And no need for weapons. All we need is nails. Cars go by. Tires go flat and the picking is easy. Even better, there are no police around so we're free to operate.

KUMIS: That's good but you still have to be on guard.

GANGSTER 3: Will do, Boss.

KUMIS: Alright, you can go know.

(*The* GANGSTERS *leave. He screams at* BLEKI.)

Ouch, damn it. Is that a massage or torture.

(*Hearing* KUMIS *scream, the* GANGSTERS *return, frightened.*)

KUMIS: I could wring your neck, you numbskull.

BLEKI: Sorry, boss, I was just getting into it is all.

KUMIS: (*To the* GANGSTERS) What are you waiting for? Scram! When I want you, I'll call.

(*After the* GANGSTERS *leaves, he motions for* ROIMA *to come closer.*)

So, Roima, how are you doing. Do you like working with me.

ROIMA: It's okay.

KUMIS: Okay? Just okay? You haven't even been here a year yet and another you're in charge of security for the whole metropolitan area. That's real power. And you say the job's okay?

(*Reflectively*) Well, I guess many [maybe?] it is just okay. If we were really successful, we'd be rolling in dough, but for the past three years it's been like neither this nor that, not rich, not poor.

But that's what I like about you, Roima. You take it as it comes. And you don't kiss ass like others. Let's not even talk about Bleki; he doesn't count. He started as an ass wipe and he's still an ass wipe.

But we have to work harder. I want to go national. Hell, I want to be an international-class bandit.

Being just one of the top gangsters in Jakarta ain't enough. That's nothing to be proud of. We have to work harder. Yeah, I'll have to work harder. (*Laughing.*)

(BLEKI *laughs with him.* KUMIS *then exits, followed by* ROIMA *and* BLEKI.)

LIGHTS CHANGE

18

Evening. A park in the center of the city. The park is a large and pleasant one, in the middle of which is an oversized clock made from grass and flowers. Flags wave in the air. Stone benches dot the corners of the park. And there is a large fountain as well, whose spray is illuminated by different colored lights. There, the SALESMAN *is attempting to sell his wares.*

SALESMAN: For God's sake, my friends, cockroaches are dangerous. Haven't you ever read anything? If there is a nuclear war, the only thing that will survive is the cockroach, a species of animal with incredible power of endurance.

So, believe me, we have to wipe out cockroaches before they wipe out us. I beg you therefore to buy my insecticide!

(JULINI *enters and stands beside the clock. She's nervous. The* SALESMAN *looks her up and down.)*

JULINI: What are you looking at me for? No way I'm going to buy that bug spray of yours. I'm a cockroach, too. So why should I buy an anti-me spray?

SALESMAN: I should have known. It's always the same, wherever I go. Rejection and refusal is all I get. But I refuse to give up hope.

This anti-cockroach spray of mine is effective and efficient! The cockroach revolution is coming! Buy my spray before it's too late. Cockroach spray! (*Exits.*)

(ROIMA *rushes in.*)

JULINI: (*Greeting him enthusiastically*) Roima!

ROIMA: Sorry, I'm in a hurry; I can't stay too long. Tell me what you want. Don't beat around the bush. If it's money, here, take this. I have work to do.

JULINI: Is that what you think I want? Money? Oh, Roima, what's the meaning of money?

What I need, darling, is attention and affection. But you're never at home; you're always working. Well, if I have an affair, don't blame me. People start to mess around because they're lonely, you know. And I am lonely. Our mattress is growing cold, honey, because you're never home. Where do you go? It seems like we never get a chance to talk about things anymore, just the two of us alone. Why, oh, why?

ROIMA: What are you talking about? You're crazy. I'm working. You know that. I'm working for you. And we're better off than we used to be. You have nice clothes now, not those smelly ones you used to wear. And you have necklaces, bracelets and rings, even if they are imitation. And that's because I'm working.

JULINI: But we never go out anymore. We never swoon beneath the silvery moon. You never tell me you love me anymore. Why? Do you have a new girlfriend?

ROIMA: Don't be crazy. I'm in a hurry. I don't have time for this.

JULINI: Now you say you don't have time. Remember how it used to be when we could spend the whole day lying in the grass and looking at the sky? Now, in the morning, you're out. Work, you say. And in the afternoon. And at night, too. Let's not even talk about the nights... come evening, you're already gone. What time is it? It's only...

(*She looks at her watch and then the grass clock.*)

That stupid thing is fucked. My watch says 5:15.

(*The grass clock does appear to be stuck as its hands read 7:30.*)

What time do you have?

ROIMA: Six o'clock.

JULINI: Which is right?

ROIMA: That one for sure; the city government made it.

JULINI: Why have you changed, darling? Take pity on me. I'll always be faithful no matter what happens.

ROIMA: I haven't changed, you idiot; I'm working. I want to be rich so that no one can step on me again, I don't want to live in the gutter. I want a house, a real one, not the one we have now. Hell, the doghouse of a government official is better than the one we live in.

JULINI: Maybe so, but does that mean you have to neglect me?

ROIMA: Can't you understand? We have to sacrifice for the future. For our future. Here's the money. (*Exits.*)

JULINI: Oh, darling... He's getting harder to hold on to. When we were poor and we wanted to go somewhere, he always told me where he was going. If this is the way it's going to be, I'd rather be what we used to be. Oh, my God, my God, why has it come to this?

(*She cries as she sings "Flowers in Mourning."*)

The beautiful memories torment me
It's hard to erase their sweet impression
The warmth of his kiss and his embrace
His flashing eyes and honeyed smile.
All the sweet nothings, the little gestures
It's so hard to forget, so hard.

Wind, I beg your service
Carry my message to him
This bundle of longing
Each night I think only of him

In each word his name I hear
In every mirror only his image I see.

The more I try to forget, the more it hurts
The more I'm shut out, the more I crave.
The sun sets, the sun rises
Evening falls, nighttime comes
All that's left are tears
And bitter sorrow in my heart.

This is the song of a flower in mourning
A song of never ending love
This is the song of a flower in mourning
A song of the neglected home.

(*Crying, she throws away the money that* ROIMA *gave her.*)

Money is necessary, sure, but love is what I need. (*Pauses*)
But money has its use, too.

(*She pick up the money then exits sadly.*)

LIGHTS CHANGE

19

Evening. In a quiet part of the city. TIBAL *is yelling at* TUMINAH *who is in tears and sobbing.* ROIMA *is standing by to make sure that* TIBAL *doesn't beat his sister.*

The monuments that dot the skyline look like silent monsters reaching for the sky.

TIBAL: God damn it, God damn it! You little bitch. Where's your backbone? Who did I kill that guy for, if not for you? Who did I go to jail for? And for what? Goddamn son of a bitch!

I should have killed you, too.

TUMINAH: Tibal...

ROIMA: Calm down, Tibal. Calm down.

TIBAL: Keep your nose out of this.

ROIMA: This is all our business. Tuminah helped me once and it's my duty to protect her.

TIBAL: (*To* TUMINAH) Oh, so that's why you're still a whore—because you got a pimp to protect you? Is he the one who turned you into a whore?

TUMINAH: No. Listen to me. With you in jail, how was I supposed to live? Who was going to take care of me? I might have lost my future, but I didn't want to die. I had to survive, even if it meant being a whore.

After all the dead ends I found, that was the only way. Go ahead, be angry if you like, but try to think about what I was supposed to do. I'm not very smart. I was here in Jakarta alone. Where was I supposed to go? Home? Where's home? I had no one.

TIBAL: Crap! What a bunch of bullshit! Sounds like a cheap film. Life's so hard you become a whore. God gives you choices. Being a whore is only one of them. If you didn't want to be a whore, you wouldn't have become one. Why did you choose that?

ROIMA: If God gives us choice, then why did you choose to kill a man and go to jail? You're the one who's irresponsible. You were selfish, thinking only about yourself. You're a man.... Well, big deal! Try being a woman. Put yourself in Tuminah's place, I'd like to see what you'd do.

TIBAL: I killed for her. Everything I did was for her.

ROIMA:	No. You were thinking about yourself.
TIBAL:	And you?
ROIMA:	Do you think Tuminah likes being a prostitute? She has dreams too. She's able to earn her own living. And now you come back. For what? To mess up her life again? Forget what's happened; the future is more important.
	Go ahead, kill her and go back to prison again. And then ask yourself, for what? We're nobodies, Tibal. We always get the short end of the stick. And if you can't keep a cool head, you'll end up even worse off. Think of the people who beat us down. They don't act that way. They're level-headed; always planning each and every move. If you want to win, you have to be calm. Figure out your moves. A little trickery comes in handy, too. You have to use strategy.
	(TIBAL *finally appears to understand what* ROIMA *is trying to tell him and now turns his anger towards himself.*)
TIBAL:	(*In tears*) All I did was for nothing. Nobody thinks of the sacrifice I made. Son of a bitch, son of a bitch!
TUMINAH:	That's not true. I respect you for what you did. If you want, we can start from scratch again. I have some money saved.
TIBAL:	I don't want any of your tainted money. Roima's right. We were born losers and no matter what we do, we'll always be losers. Well, I don't care anymore; I know what I have to do. That much is clear. If you're going to lose anyway, you might as well go down fighting. Goodbye, Tuminah...
TUMINAH:	Where are you going? I can stop working tomorrow. We can go wherever we want to go. We can be together again.
TIBAL:	Whether I go to jail or not, I don't care. I know what I have to do. (*To* ROIMA) If you like Tuminah, take care of her. I'm going... (*Exits quickly.*)

TUMINAH: He's gone. Roima... I'm afraid he's going to do something terrible.

ROIMA: I know what he's going to do but it would be useless to try to stop him.

TUMINAH: What? What's he going to do, Roima?

ROIMA: Who destroyed your life?

TUMINAH: Kumis.

(JULINI appears but, seeing ROIMA and TUMINAH together quickly conceals herself. She is jealous.)

ROIMA: Right. So he's going to find Kumis and kill him.

TUMINAH: *(Frightened)* He'll get himself killed first. Look at all the men that Kumis has. We have to stop him.

ROIMA: It's useless.

TUMINAH: *(Embracing ROIMA)* What can we do, Roima? For God's sake, what can we do?

(TUMINAH cries in ROIMA's arms. At first he is stiff but then he returns her embrace and strokes her hair lovingly. JULINI sees this and grows more jealous. She tries to restrain herself.)

ROIMA: Don't be frightened. I'll always be here. I'll protect you, forever.

(Unable to restrain herself any longer, JULINI jumps out from her hiding place.)

JULINI: Protect you? Protect you? Oh my God. What about me? It's over. My world is destroyed. The earth is shaking; the sky is falling; stars are dropping from the sky. Oh my God! I am heartbroken. I have been kicked aside; pushed into a ravine.

(ROIMA and TUMINAH are startled and stunned.)

So this is your extra work, is it? Plugging a slut. Busy, you tells me. Sure. Busy with your new girlfriend! Oh, woe is me! Woe, woe, woe! It's over. I'm bereft. Can I ever believe a man again? They're all snakes, mules, lice, cockroaches, all of them! Oh, it's over.

(*Crying,* JULINI *she starts to exit.*)

ROIMA: Wait, Jul. Julini! (*To* TUMINAH) Go to Tarsih's. We'll meet there. I have to straighten this out with Julini. (*Running after* JULINI) Julini...!

(*So stunned is* TUMINAH, *she seems not to know what to do. Suddenly,* JULINI *appears from a different direction.*)

JULINI: How could you do this to me, Tuminah? My own friend stabbing me in the back. How could you do it? It's all over... I never thought... I never guessed that my boyfriend would be stolen by my own best friend. Oh, oh, oh...

(*She exits again, leaving* TUMINAH *truly confused.*)

TUMINAH: Damn, damn, damn! (*Exits.*)

LIGHTS CHANGE

20

Evening. At JULINI'*s and* ROIMA'*s home. The house has been much improved since its former state. There is now some furniture—though the décor is still in questionable test[taste].* ROIMA *and* JULINI *have had an argument and* JULINI *is now near to hysteria, crying and screaming.* ROIMA *is trying his best to calm her down.)*

ROIMA: Listen to me, idiot. Shut up for a second.

JULINI: (*Crying, screaming*) No, no, I won't! How could you forget what we've gone through together? Now that you have some money, you find someone younger. How could you forget the promise we made? Now that you have some money, our world has been turned upside down. This is the fate of the world's transexuals. Rubber sandals is what we are. When they're worn out, you get thrown away.

ROIMA: Stop your whining! You don't know what you're talking about. All of that...

JULINI: (*Pointedly*) Maybe I'm a whiner. Maybe I don't know anything. Maybe I'm stupid. Maybe I never could satisfy you in bed. But I love you. Can't you feel that? My heart is broken shattered and scattered in bits and pieces. It is dust, taken by the wind. Oh, it hurts. It hurts.

            Where is a knife, a razor? I want to kill myself.

ROIMA: Calm down, stupid. Be quiet!

JULINI: What did I do wrong? I took care of you when you were poor. I gave you everything I had, everything you wanted. Blue jeans, a LaCoste shirt, Nike shoes, Guci glasses, everything. All imported. I always bought the best cologne for you. Underarm spray, too, and Madonna shampoo. Everything! So what if I had only soy sauce for my rice as long as you had meat? When you wanted *tempe*, I made you *tempe*. What did I do wrong?

ROIMA: For God's sake, are you going to listen or not?

JULINI: No I'm not! And in bed, I did whatever you wanted me to do. Even when I was tired, if you nudged me, I was yours. What did I do wrong? How can I ever face another morning? Where's a rope? A rope! I want a rope to hang myself!

ROIMA: Crazy little motherfucker! God, you make me mad.

            (ROIMA *slaps* JULINI. *She is shocked and upset.*)

JULINI: And now you dare to slap me!

It's over, all right. I thought maybe it was only half over. We'll divorce. Divorce me! I beg you for a divorce.

ROIMA: I can't divorce you. We aren't married! And you know why, don't you? Because we're both men, that's why. And we can't have children either. I thought you accepted that. So now, what are you doing? I'm a man, you know. I can still get excited by a naked woman. I'm a man. I'm not a tranny.

JULINI: Well I am! You've always known that. If you hate me for that now, why didn't you then?

How can you do this? How can you throw away the light of the silvery moon? You've deceived me.

If you didn't want me, I could have found another gigolo. There are tons who would love to corabbitate with me.

It's only now, after you're rich, you can say that. Now, after meeting Tuminah. Now, that you've found out her twat is juicier than mine.

ROIMA: This has nothing to do with twat, you fool. This is different.

JULINI: No it's not. You've betrayed our love. We're getting a divorce!

(JULINI *throws her belongings into a suitcase and goes.*)

ROIMA: Where are you going?

JULINI: To hell. What do you care? (*Runs away.*)

ROIMA: (*Remorsefully*) Oh, Julini, Julini…. Son a bitch!

LIGHTS DIE INSTANTLY

A MUSICAL CHORD IS HEARD

21

Night. A pick-up place for transsexual prostitutes. The TRANSWOMEN *are dressed in bewitching and glamorous apparel. They are singing, "The Song of Three Pleasures," each with her own style and voice.*

TRANSWOMEN: *What is it they're looking for?*

> *The three pleasures, my love, three pleasures*
> *The you-know-what, the mouth and the mind*
> *All three are very necessary.*
>
> *But to have them, my love*
> *The three pleasures, the three pleasures*
> *You need to have money, you need the dough*
> *There's nothing in this world for free.*
>
> *What can be sold, we sell*
> *We will do anything to live*
> *Fate is in our own hands*
> *Who else cares about us, who else?*

(Just as the song ends, the sound of whistles and sirens is heard—the sign of an impending raid. All the TRANSWOMEN *run around trying to find a place to hide. This situation is one of confusion.*

(After it is quiet for a while, the TRANSWOMEN *return to their former positions and begin to talk to one another, as if nothing had happened. But then, the sound of whistles is heard again, and the* TRANSWOMEN *go into a frenzy again.*

(It is two WATCHMEN *who are blowing the whistles. They enter along with a* MINOR GOVERNMENT OFFICIAL. *With all the* TRANSWOMEN *in hiding, the area appears to be empty but they call out for them to come out of hiding.*

(The TRANSWOMEN *gather again, grumbling and commenting among themselves as they do. When they see it is not the police, just the two* WATCHMEN

and the MINOR OFFICIAL *whom they know, they speak more raucously and cynically.*)

MINOR OFFICIAL: (*Trying to get the* TRANSWOMEN *to calm down*) Listen to me, ladies. Listen to me.

(*Because the* TRANSWOMEN *won't stop talking and listen to him, the* MINOR OFFICIAL *signals to one of the* WATCHMEN *to take his place.*)

You talk to them. I can't get them to shut up. (*Steps aside.*)

WATCHMAN 1: (*Loudly*) Listen to me, ladies! If you don't want to listen, then I will shoot this gun of mine. Don't blame me if one of you gets shot! (*Screaming*) Bang!

(*The* TRANSWOMEN *scream but then, finally, are silent.*)

Listen to me, girls. This concerns your future. It's important. I'm sure that all of you look in the mirror every day. But some time try looking at yourself more closely. Have you no shame?

TRANSWOMAN 1: If you mean that thing down there between our legs, honey, we have no use for that except to piss.

MINOR OFFICIAL: This isn't a joke. In the framework of mental development, all behavior that offends public sensibilities must be eradicated, especially amoral behavior like your own. Being a tranny is sinful enough, but you top it off by being a prostitute.

TRANSWOMAN 3: Don't get high-and-mighty with me. Like all those military officers in government positions, I am a "dual-function" worker, too. During the day, I'm a butcher but at night I put on my dress to earn some extra money. I have five children, almost all of them in college. My wife knows what I do at night. It's a profession!

WATCHMAN 1: Isn't there anything else you could do?

TRANSWOMAN 3: If I were a civil servant, corruption would be a possibility, but I'm not. So what else? Steal? That's against the law!

WATCHMAN 1: Prostitution is against the law, too, don't you know?! And that's why I'm here; to remind you of that while there is still time. Come to your senses. This is amoral. And in the framework of mental and spiritual development...

TRANSWOMAN 1: What in the world are you talking about, going around in circles like that? Mental-spiritual, mental-spiritual.... If you want to try one of us just ask. You don't have to beat around the bush with all this talking. Do you have any money?

MINOR OFFICIAL: Listen to me. In a few months the city will be building a terminal cable car terminal here. I'm only here to warn you to be ready while there is still time.

TRANSWOMAN 2: Big deal. You want to erect a terminal, go ahead and erect one. That's your business. We deal with other kind of erections.

WATCHMAN 1: Once again, this kind of practice will be forbidden. And if you insist on engaging in this kind of behavior, then you'll have to deal with the law. You have to realize this and follow the right path.

(JULINI *enters looking depressed.*)

JULINI: What's going on?

TRANSWOMAN 5: What's-his-face is practicing how to give a speech.

WATCHMAN 1: Oh, you trannies, think of the ever-after, and the fires of hell. Do not continue to accumulate sins. Your way of life is pestilence and pestilence is contagious.

TRANSWOMAN 1: Don't insult us, man. We are not a disease? We hang here and guys pick us up. It's all voluntary; there's no force. If you don't like us, that's no problem. We don't care.

TRANSWOMAN 2: That's right! (*To the others*) I wonder if he's a front guy for some big shot. There's something fishy about him. It's like he's intentionally trying to stir up trouble.

TRANSWOMAN 3: You're right. If he were serious, he wouldn't talk so much. He just comes, hands you the warrant and bang bang bang.

TRANSWOMAN 1: Bang bang bang!? This isn't police headquarters, you know.

TRANSWOMAN 3: I didn't mean bang-bang-bang; I meant they'd put us in cuffs.

TRANSWOMAN 2: Let's beat 'em up!

TRANSWOMAN 3: Yeah, let's whip 'em!

TRANSWOMAN 4: Hang 'em! Teach 'em a lesson.

TRANSWOMAN 5: Cut off their dicks...! But do they still have dicks?

(*With all the commotion, the atomosphere grows tense. The two* WATCHMEN *stand ready with their pistols. The* MINOR OFFICIAL *looks frightened.*)

MINOR OFFICIAL: Calm down! Calm down and listen to me.

TRANSWOMAN 3: We'll calm down when you're in the grave.

TRANSWOMAN 1: This is our place! Get out of here!

TRANSWOMAN 2: Let's get him!

TRANSWOMAN 4: Cut their necks!

TRANSWOMAN 2: Kill him!

(*The* TRANSWOMEN *attack the* MINOR OFFICIAL. JULINI *stands to the side, not joining in, completely unaffected by the state of affairs.*)

MINOR OFFICIAL: Help me, help! Get out your guns! Don't just stand there!

(The WATCHMEN *fire their pistols. Two shots ring out and the* TRANSWOMEN *disperse. Another set of shots ring out.*

(JULINI *clutches her chest to find it wet with blood. She is startled and in pain. She starts to faint.*)

JULINI: It's blood. Oh my God... Is this real? It's not tomato sauce? (*Tasting the blood with her fingers*) Oh, my God, it is blood. It's really blood. I'm a goner. It's the end. I'm kicking the bucket.

(*As* JULINI *falls* ROIMA *enters.*)

WATCHMAN 1: I killed her. I'm a murderer. Did the bullet come from my gun? No, it couldn't have. I have rubber bullets. It must have come from yours.

WATCHMAN 2: No, it came from yours. There was smoke coming out of your gun. If it were my gun, she'd still be alive. I have empty shells. See. You're the murderer.

WATCHMAN 1: No, it was you.

WATCHMAN 2: It was you.

ROIMA: Julini.... Jul.

JULINI: You were looking for me? Do you still love me?

ROIMA: Don't talk. We'll get you to the hospital. You're wounded bad.

JULINI: There's no time. I want to die just like in a film. I want to die in my lover's arms. In times like this when you are near me, I am so happy.

ROIMA: God's sake, stop talking. You'll bleed worse.

JULINI: I don't care. I am so happy. Goodbye, Roima. Goodbye, comrades. I have to go. Up there, in that big park in the sky, I'll see what I can do about you down here. I'll take our case to the heavenly courts. My dear audience, I have to die now. This is wonderful.

(JULINI *expires.* ROIMA *stares at the two* WATCHMEN *and then the* MINOR OFFICIAL. *The* TRANSWOMEN *follow suit. Readying themselves to attack, they advance slowly towards the three.*)

MINOR OFFICIAL: Run!

(*He flees and is followed by the* WATCHMEN. *The* TRANSWOMEN *start to chase them but stop when looking back to see* ROIMA *bowed before* JULINI'*s body.*)

TRANSWOMAN 1: What are we going to do, Roima? What can we do?

ROIMA: Why did it have to be her?

TRANSWOMAN 2: Yes, why her? She wasn't doing anything. She just happened to be here and then the bullet went astray and entered her chest.

TRANSWOMAN 4: Is a rubber bullet sharp?

TRANSWOMAN 5: Well, if it killed her, it must have been sharp enough?

TRANSWOMAN 3: That's now beside the point. We're not going to let this rest. We'll report this to the governor or even to Parliament; to the Minister of Women's Affairs, to the Legal Rights Association, the National Council on Human Rights. Remember the Malang River tragedy? Now it's happened again. We can't let this keep on happening. We're citizens too. We have identity cards and pay taxes. We have to report it. Julini was a good person, a friend of us all. She was good…

(*She starts to cry and then the other* TRANSWOMEN *cry too, their voices a medley of eerie sounds. At this moment*

JULINI's spirit rises from her body, like a bird, and moves to a more comfortable sleeping position elsewhere.)

JULINI: What a racket. When trannies cry, they certainly do it loudly! Slack lips from too much exercise, I suspect. (*Goes back to sleep.*)

TRANSWOMAN 1: Julini was our heroine.

TRANSWOMAN 2: Our pride.

TRANSWOMAN 4: Our idol. The best transwoman of 1985!

TRANSWOMAN 3: This sadism has to stop. Just because we don't have power behind us, they go after us and stomp on us and kill us.

ROIMA: (*Shouting*) We'll go to that government official's home.

(*Everyone shouts in approval.*)

TRANSWOMAN 3: Wait! Today is a day of historical importance for trans women, both professionals and amateurs. We shall proclaim this day "National Transpeople's Day." We'll erect a statue of Julini as a reminder for the next generation of transpeople that there once took place here a tragic and bloody event of which Julini was the victim.

ROIMA: (*Shouting again*) Let's go to the official's house.

TRANSWOMAN 1: She was our prima donna.

TRANSWOMAN 2: A reflection of our fate.

TRANSWOMAN 3: Why did she have to die? Why, oh why?

(*All go in the direction of the* HIGH OFFICIAL's *home. The music blares and everyone falls in step.*)

ROIMA: (*Screaming*) There's his house now!

22

Night. The home of the HIGH OFFICIAL. ROIMA, *the* TRANSWOMEN *and* JULINI*'s spirit stand in a group. The* HIGH OFFICIAL *receives the crowd in his expansive living room*

HIGH OFFICIAL: Tell those who want to come in, to come in.

ROIMA: We're all here, sir.

HIGH OFFICIAL: Oh, so are you? Well, get on with it. Tell me what you have to say. My time is precious and it's late at night? What other government official would be willing to see people like you at this time of time. Come on, speak up.

ROIMA: She wanted only to live. She never bothered anyone, never used force. She did what she did because she was hungry. She was working, so that she didn't starve. Maybe she was trash. All she could do was massage. Destiny threw her into the gutter and had she lived until a ripe old age, that is where she would have stayed, clustered with the lice and cockroaches.

We're nobodies. Our only problem is how to fill our stomachs. So why was she shot dead?

HIGH OFFICIAL: Alright already but get to the point. What do you want?

ROIMA: We demand legal action and an equal sentence for the man who shot her.

TRANSWOMAN 1: And a Julini Monument.

TRANSWOMAN 2: A Julini Plaza!

TRANSWOMAN 3: A Julini Award.

TRANSWOMAN 4: Some basic supplies would be good.

TRANSWOMAN 5: Julini Boulevard!

(*The* TRANSWOMEN *vie to state their opinion.*)

HIGH OFFICIAL: Quiet down! Quiet! (*The group quiets down*) Thank you.

OK, we will study your report but you will have to wait until we finish processing this case. Whoever is at fault will not escape the law. As for your other demands, you'll have to wait for a decision on those.

ROIMA: How long will we have to wait?

HIGH OFFICIAL: Trust me. I am a leader who was chosen by the people. I wasn't appointed to my position. I always finish every case completely and fairly. Is that understood?

(*No one answers.*)

Alright, you may go now. I need my rest after a long day of working for the people.

(*They exit, but with uncertainty, JULINI scampers to follow them.*)

JULINI: (*Flying like a bird*) Hey, hey, hey.... Don't leave me behind.

LIGHTS CHANGE

23

Morning. Home of the HIGH OFFICIAL *a few hours later. The* HIGH OFFICIAL *is angry and has ordered the* MINOR OFFICIAL *and the two* WATCHMEN *to come to see him.*

HIGH OFFICIAL: Get in here, you idiots.

(*The* WATCHMEN *enter, looking pale*)

You stupid fools. When are you going to learn to use your brains? Now what are we to do with you? I wonder how you'll like prison?

WATCHMAN 1: No, but it was your man who told us to shoot.

HIGH OFFICIAL: Shoot fine, but not with your gun. Why didn't you use your hands or your feet or your billy clubs? You're better at that.

WATCHMAN 1: But they started to attack us, sir.

HIGH OFFICIAL: You should have screamed at them. People in groups are cowards. They would have backed down. Heavy handed is fine as long as you aren't heavy fingered, not with a pistol, anyway.

(WATCHMAN 1 *leaves the room momentarily. Apparently, someone has called him.*)

WATCHMAN 2: Sir, there are five reporters waiting to see you.

HIGH OFFICIAL: What do they want?

WATCHMAN 1: They said they want an explanation about the tranny killings.

HIGH OFFICIAL: Killings? Where did the plural come from? There was only one killed. God forbid if the media has found out what happened. That would be disastrous.

MINOR OFFICIAL: Disastrous for all of us, sir.

HIGH OFFICIAL: That's right; all of us. Fools! Tell them I have a fever and that I'll send word when I can receive visitors.

WATCHMAN 2: Yes, sir. (*Exits.*)

HIGH OFFICIAL: Not even twenty-four hours and everyone's up in arms. It's hard work being an official. It might look nice from the outside but I never get enough sleep and I'm always the target of criticism. And, in this case, this clearly wasn't even my fault.

WATCHMAN 2: (*Coming back in with a newspaper in hand*) Here's the evening paper, sir. There's a full report on the Julini shooting.

HIGH OFFICIAL: Don't they have anything else to write about? Look at how fast this thing is spreading. My God, look at that photo. This is going to make people upset. How could they take a picture like this? I'm suspicious. It seems to me that there's someone behind this. This could be a frame-up. Go and chase those reporters out of here.

WATCHMAN 1: Yes, sir. (*Exits.*)

HIGH OFFICIAL: Is that tranny really dead?

WATCHMAN 2: Yes, sir. I saw with my own eyes.

HIGH OFFICIAL: Oh, hell. So am I now supposed to pay for your mistakes? (*Reading the newspaper out loud*) "Julini's friends are asking that a statue be erected in her honor.... The movement has found support from various factions, including...." Oh, for crying out loud! Look at who's pledged his support. My political opponent! Boy, that's fishing in muddy waters! He just wants a free ride to popularity.

MINOR OFFICIAL: Might I make a suggestion, sir?

HIGH OFFICIAL: Fire away!

MINOR OFFICIAL: Thank you. sir. If I may suggest, sir, in order to appear more sympathetic to public sentiment, if they want a monument, give it to them. If a statue is what they want, it's theirs. There's a lot to gain from this, sir. First of all, it would cool their tempers and second we would be lauded as officials who are sensitive to public feelings.

HIGH OFFICIAL: Maybe you're right. A statue, a monument. For God's sake, that's our specialty anyway. But for now, get out. I don't want to see your face around here again.

(*They exit but then* WATCHMAN 1 *re-enters.*)

WATCHMAN 2: Sir, the reporters won't leave.

HIGH OFFICIAL: Find a way to make them leave. Chase them out, if necessary.

WATCHMAN 2: What should I use, sir? My billy club or my pistol?

HIGH OFFICIAL: I don't care. Use whatever is necessary as long as you don't shoot anyone

WATCHMAN 1: Yes, sir. (*Exits.*)

HIGH OFFICIAL: This incident could ruin my reputation.

(WATCHMAN 1 *enters again, trembling.*)

HIGH OFFICIAL: Now what do you want?

WATCHMAN 1: There are representatives from the Union of Legal Scholars and the Chair of the IPA...

HIGH OFFICIAL: The Indonesian Press Association?

WATCHMAN 1: The Indonesian People-Like-Us Association, And also representatives from Legal Aid Institute, the Consumer's League, the Environmental Protection Association, CNN, and the National Bonsai Association too, sir.

HIGH OFFICIAL: (*Confounded*) What do they have to do with this?

WATCHMAN 1: I didn't ask, sir.

(WATCHMAN 2 *re-renters hastily.*)

WATCHMAN 1: Sir, there's a delegation from the Minister of Social Affairs along with representatives from the Ministry of Women's Affairs, the Ministry of Culture and Education, and the Attorney General's Office!

HIGH OFFICIAL: (*Weakly*) All right. I give up. We'll build a statue if that's what they want. We'll build a monument, a statue and whatever-the-fuck!

LIGHTS CHANGE

24

Afternoon. A plaza, the site of a newly constructed Julini Monument. The plaza is ready to be officially opened. With a background of festive music, ROIMA *and a group of* TRANSWOMEN *carry a covered statue of* JULINI *into the plaza.*

All the SLUM DWELLERS *are present as are the* HIGH OFFICIAL, *the* MINOR OFFICIAL *and the* WATCHMAN.

The statue is placed in the center of the plaza. A salvo is fired as the HIGH OFFICIAL *advances to the podium.*

HIGH OFFICIAL: After a fierce struggle at the upper echelons of power, praise the Lord, your request to erect a statue in our heroine's honor was granted. For months I struggled with the decision of what kind of ceremony would please all interested parties until finally we arrive at this historic day. For that we are thankful.

The monument we have erected is built on a foundation of love and affection. I won't say much more but this is a unique event. I am happy today and hope that you are happy, too.

ALL: Amen.

HIGH OFFICIAL: I hereby officially commemorate the erection of this statue.

(*Another salvo is fired. The* MINOR OFFICIAL *gives the* HIGH OFFICIAL *a large pair of scissors to cut the ribbon, but the scissors are blunt and he is unable to cut the ribbon.*)

Give me a knife. Where's a knife?

(*The* MINOR OFFICIAL *scrambles to find a knife. After finding one, he gives it to the* HIGH OFFICIAL. *The* HIGH OFFICIAL *angrily hacks at the ribbon and finally manages to cut it. Everyone claps as the cloth falls from the statue of* JULINI.)

Now we shall have a moment of silence in honor of the person in whose honor this monument was erected. Please stand everyone. Let the moment of silence begin.

(*During this moment of silence, the* HIGH OFFICIAL *gives* TUMINAH *the eye. He then says something to the* WATCHMEN *who then go to stand beside* TUMINAH.)

The moment of silence is over.

(*The statue is now uncovered completely. The statue of* JULINI *bears an exact resemblance to the person and everyone present, the* TRANSWOMEN *especially, begin to cry.*)

This ceremony is now ended. For those who want to continue to cry, please carry on in your own homes. Now you are dismissed.

WATCHMAN 2: (*To* TUMINAH) The boss wants to see you at the regular place.

TUMINAH: Fine.

WATCHMAN 2: Now.

TUMINAH: Alright.

WATCHMAN 2: Follow me. (*They exit.*)

(*The* HIGH OFFICIAL *exits.* ROIMA *stands below* JULINI*'s statue, looking at it in silence. Everyone exits.*)

LIGHTS CHANGE

25

Night. At the Julini Monument. ROIMA *is still staring at the statue of* JULINI *and talking to himself.*

ROIMA: And it the last moments of your life, I was bad to you. I was ungrateful. I slapped you and wanted to throw you out. You were so good and I was so bad. I was stupid, a fool, a liar. I'm so sorry.

(JULINI*'s spirit speaks to* ROIMA *but, of course, he is unable to hear her speak.*)

JULINI: There's not much good in feeling sorry afterwards.

ROIMA: Yes, I was attracted to Tuminah, and she was to me. But that's as far as it went. Then you got jealous and angry. You wouldn't listen to what I had to say.

JULINI: Where there's smoke, there's love; that's a sign. And your love is like water wetting the leaves of the rose bush and falling into the gutter.... No, no, that's not right.

ROIMA: We're nobodies. People like us shouldn't fight. The end is always the same; one of us is always sacrificed.

JULINI: How true! Without fuel, the fire dies. When two elephants fight, someone else steals their tusks and the shrubs between them can only winge.

ROIMA: I was mad at you, at myself, the situation, fate, poverty, everything. But why did you have to be the one? Why you, when you didn't do anything?

(Angrily, he sings the song "The Angry Frog.")

What good is it for a frog to be angry
When the world is so large?
A hollow croak in the middle of night
Its echo vanishes with no meaning.

Humans are no more than a flock of chickens
With the bigger pecking on the smaller
The small pecking on the even smaller
And so on and on it goes.

This is the song of the angry frog
The song of dreams, of wasted effort.
But the world must soon change
Until there are no poor anymore.

JULINI: Oh, like a night owl pining for that time of the month. Ah, wrong again.

(Suddenly, in the distance shouting is heard.)

KUMIS OS: *(Screaming)* Help! Don't, Tibal, don't!

TIBAL OS: I finally found you, the cancer of it all. Now you are dead.

KUMIS OS: Help! Don't!

ROIMA: God damn it! I can't let him do it. Shit *(Running towards the sound of the voices.)*

JULINI: *(Relaxing from her upright position)* This being a statue thing is tiring. Whoever said being a statue was fun?

LIGHTS CHANGE

26

Night. Julini Plaza. As JULINI *in the form of a statue is resting, the world suddenly darkens. Thunder erupts.* JULINI*'s statue is startled. Then she becomes even more startled when monuments from around Jakarta convene at the plaza: the monkey king* HANUMAN, *who, as depicted in the monument that was erected at Pancoran traffic circle is ready to fly into space to resist aggressors from the North; a* SOLDIER-FARMER *and a* FARMER'S WIFE, *as depicted in the Hero of the People Monument on Menteng Raya; a* YOUNG MAN *and* WOMAN, *who are carrying a bouquet of flowers, as is depicted in the Friendship Monument (also known as the "Welcome Monument") located at the Hotel Indonesia traffic circle; a* CARRIER OF THE FLAME, *as is depicted in the Spirit of Youth Monument located at the Senayan traffic circle; a* MAN WITH CHAINS, *as is depicted in the Irian Jaya Freedom Monument located in Banteng Square; and others.* JULINI *stares in wonder at them all.*

JULINI: What the...? Are you...?

HANUMAN: Yes, I'm from Pancoran. I was supposed to go to outer space but never got off the ground. The takeoff pad is much too small.

SOLDIER-FARMER: Howdy! I'm from Menteng Raya. Sure did surprise me when they outfitted me with a rifle; I should have had a hoe. I can't even use this thing. If you tell me to shoot my foot, I'd probably hit my head.

FARMER'S WIFE: That rifle gives me the willies. I told him before. Don't go, Pop. Who'll look after our rice field? Look my basket. It's empty. We all need rice. But no, he always tells me, "This is what's been programmed." Nope, I never have understood.

YOUNG MAN AND WOMAN: Welcome, welcome.

CARRIER OF THE FLAME: Ha ha! Well they have me eating fire every day. Think about it. Fire! Do you think I like that? They don't even give me clothes to wear. I suppose they think statues don't get colds. No, those people who made us didn't know what they were doing.

MAN IN CHAINS: And look at me with these chains. They're heavy, you know. I'd rather be eating cake in this position. Better that than having to yell "Freedom" all the time. Who hears me anyway? Find me some proof, Freedom, shit! Look at me. I still have my chains.

JULINI: So you are statues?

YOUNG MAN and WOMAN: Welcome, welcome

HANUMAN: In line with tradition, whenever a new monument is erected in Jakarta, we gather to introduce ourselves. We are all from JSA, the Jakarta Statuary Association.

CARRIER OF THE FLAME: I'm sorry but not everyone could come. Prince Diponegoro from Monas Square, well his horse has the flu and he gets motion sickness when he takes the bus so he sends his regards. And Gajah Mada, too. His feet suddenly swelled up.

SOLDIER-FARMER: Well that's the way they made him, with big feet.

CARRIER OF THE FLAME: But they're even bigger now. He's been standing too long, I suppose. At any rate, the best of luck to you from all the statues that couldn't attend.

YOUNG MAN and WOMAN: Welcome, welcome

JULINI: Yeah, yeah...

FARMER'S WIFE: Tell me, Julini, why'd they make a statue of you?

JULINI: I don't know, ma'am. All of a sudden I was lying there with a bullet in me. I never thought I'd be made into a statue. I'm just an ordinary person. I had hoped that whoever it was who shot me would be brought to justice, but from what I can see, he's still running around free. And then they made me into this. Funny, huh?

SOLDIER-FARMER: That's the world for all of us, huh, Ma?

FARMER'S WIFE: Talk about funny. Look at the policeman pocketing a five thousand note over there. But why not? Can you blame him? The traffic offender gets away without having to go to court and the policeman has some food for his next meal. Just funny, is all.

It's nice being a statue at an intersection; there are all kinds of things to see. Yup, we're witness to many incidents but can't do anything. We're statues.. And we see it all the time, Jul, all the time.

CARRIER OF THE FLAME: As statue we see lots of things to laugh about but we can't laugh.

HANUMAN: If we could laugh, who'd believe it? They'd think it was magic. (*Laughing.*)

JULINI: I've not seen anything to laugh about.

(*Suddenly the sound of shouting is heard.*)

MAN IN CHAINS: Hey, there's somebody coming. Back in your positions.

(*The* STATUES *return to their proper positions.* KUMIS *enters, stumbling, his chest covered with blood. He is followed by* TIBAL, *who holds a knife in his hand.*)

KUMIS: Help. I'm going to die. Where is Bleki? Roima!

TIBAL: (*Calmly*) Even if they do come you're still going to die.

(*When he waves his knife,* TIBAL *screams again.*)

Yell all you want; a lot of good it will do you. I've been waiting for the right time and now you're done for.

KUMIS: I'm already done for.

TIBAL: But I want to see how you die.

KUMIS: Help me. Take me to the hospital. I don't have any strength. Blood, I can't stand the sight of blood.

TIBAL: You're going to die and people will find your corpse. At most they'll think you're a "mystery killing" victim.

           (KUMIS *dies.*)

           Damn it, Kumis. Damn it all to hell. You died too quickly. Hmmm.... The river's a good place for him now.

           (*For a moment it is silent, then the* FARMER'S WIFE *steps down from her pedestal and ad starts to vomit.*)

JULINI: Are you pregnant, Ma'am?

FARMER'S WIFE: No, (*Coughing*) I just can't stand the sight of blood.

JULINI: There's someone else coming.

           (*The* STATUES *return to their positions.* ROIMA *enters.*)

ROIMA: There's blood. They must have come this way.

           (ROIMA *follows the blood spots until he exits. The* FARMER's WIFE *throws up again.*)

SOLDIER-FARMER: (*To his* WIFE) Get a hold of yourself, Ma.

HANUMAN: It's getting awfully busy around here; we should go.

           (*All the statues agree and exit rapidly. Then, in the distance, an alarm rings. Offstage,* PEOPLE *begin to scream* "Fire!" *They enter and begin to run about.*)

SALESMAN: (*As he passes through*) As a short-term solution, fire is even more effective than my spray. Cockroaches are turned directly into ash. But that's only a temporary solution, because those that survive breed and procreate in far greater numbers. But my spray can take care of them right down to their roots. Why won't anyone buy any? Bug spray, cockroach spray! Buy two get a third free.

LIGHTS CHANGE

27

Night. Prostitution complex and the slum. TARSIH's home is ablaze as is the entire slum. All the PROSTITUTES and all the SLUM DWELLERS are running around in fright, not knowing what to do.

TARSIH: How did this happen, Tuminah? Who set fire to our house?

TUMINAH: I don't know, I just don't know. We have to find out.

PROSTITUTES: Fire, fire!

BLEKI: (*Running about and screaming*) Kumis! Boss! Where are you?

ASNAH: Oh no! What did we do wrong?

PERSON 1:   Grab the things that can still be saved. Hurry!

PERSON 2:   It's spreading fast. Fire! Fire!

               (KASIJAH *sings, showing no sign of knowing what is happening around her.*)

KASIJAH: *We are yams*
               We are rice
               We are cows
               We are pigs.
               We are shit

PERSON 1:   What the hell is that crazy whore doing?

PERSON 2:   Save yourself first you idiot. Forget the rest. (*Running away.*)

               (*The first spreads, out of control.*)

TARSIH:	The deed to my house! My papers! Son a bitch! It's over, it's over...
TUMINAH:	Run, Tarsih. You have to get out!

(TARSIH *runs to her house which is already in flames.* TUMINAH *attempts to stop her.*)

TARSIH:	All my things! My deed! They'll evict me. (*To* TUMINAH) Let me go! My deed!
TUMINAH:	Tarsih!

(*Entering her home,* TARSIH *is trapped inside as flames consume everything.*)

BLEKI:	(*Still running around and screaming*) Kumis! Boss! Where are you?

(*The flames spread and then grow higher consuming everything in their path.*)

LIGHTS CHANGE

28

Night. Julini Monument Plaza. A few hours after the burning of the slum and prostitution complex, the new homeless have gathered beneath the JULINI *monument. They all look weak, stunned, and hopeless.*

ASNAH:	Everything's gone.
PERSON 1:	And that crazy whore, too.
TUMINAH:	And Tarsih.

(ROIMA *enters. He stares around sadly.*)

Roima...

ROIMA:	I know, I heard about it. I saw it. And it wasn't an accident either; it was set.

(TIBAL *enters bathed in blood and waving his knife in his hand.*)

TIBAL: I did it. I killed Kumis.

TUMINAH: (*Screaming*) Kumis...!

ROIMA: We have to find out about this. There are questions that have to be answered.

(*Everyone agrees and as one they rise and go to the office of the* HIGH OFFICIAL.)

LIGHTS CHANGE

29

Night. At the office of the HIGH OFFICIAL. *The* HIGH OFFICIAL *is getting ready to receive visitors. With him are the* MINOR OFFICIAL *and the two* WATCHMEN. *Anti-riot* TROOPS *in helmets and uniform are also present.*

HIGH OFFICIAL: Show in those who want to see me.

ROIMA: We're all here now, sir. We're here to ask how this catastrophe started.

HIGH OFFICIAL: (*Angrily*) How am I supposed to know? It was an accident. We will conduct an investigation and if we find anyone... we'll take him to court. But if this was an accident, what can I say? Who's to say how the fire started?

It was an accident; trust me, an accident. But I promise you that in the area that burned we'll put up better buildings. Does that make you satisfied?

ROIMA: But none of those buildings will be for us, right. That's what you wanted to begin with, wasn't it?

HIGH OFFICIAL: You insolent son of a bitch; keep you accusations to yourself. Fire can start anywhere. Don't jump to conclusions before we investigate.

ROIMA: (*Shouting*) Twice now we've been chased away, this time even more sadistically. Where are we supposed to go? We're cockroaches. We stand around waiting for an opportunity, but the chance never comes and we have to go back to our holes in the ground, back to the gutters and the outhouses where we belong.

SALESMAN: (*Elsewhere, peddling his wares*) Buy my bugs spray! This will take care of them. Cockroaches must be wiped out, down to their grandchildren. There is no way around it. If not, the cockroaches will take over. They will push us out. Buy my insecticide. It's effective against cockroaches. Don't wait until the milk is split. Don't wait for the cockroaches to push us into the grave. Don't wait for the cockroach age to come. We'll never win if we wait.

HIGH OFFICIAL: Call in the guards. This situation is getting out of hand.

(ROIMA *and the others advance slowly towards the* HIGH OFFICIAL *who is now surrounded by an antiriot squad, complete with helmets. Just as the group seems ready to attack,* ROIMA *suddenly does something unexpected.*)

ROIMA: (*Shouting*) Stop! We have gone far enough. Stop! Relax, calm down, douse the flames in your head. Cool your boiling blood. Force is not the answer.

(*The* PEOPLE *stop advancing.*)

Use your brains; not your fists and feet. It's not yet the time, my friends; it's not the time. This is not our age. Our age is tomorrow, or maybe the next day or another century away. But it will come.

That has been predicted. So wait and be patient. Shoulder the burden, however heavy it may be, without complaint.

PERSON 1: What are you talking about? What are we waiting for? Don't listen to him. Is he our leader? My fingers are itchy. We've gone this far and we have nothing left. So what if we die doing it?

(PEOPLE *start moving again but then* TIBAL *runs in front of them.*)

TIBAL: Roima is right. Better to use the brain than the knife. I just killed a man and my knife is covered with his blood. Those who don't agree with Roima, step up and I'll take care of you, too. Come on, who will step up?

HIGH OFFICIAL: (*Shouting*) What is this, a discussion on the battlefield? Do you want to fight or not? Come on. I'm ready. Stop your jabbering. The trigger is cocked. All that's left is the bang.

Come on, step forward and die.

ROIMA: Don't worry. We're not going to do anything. We'll go back to the place where we belong, if that is what you want us to do.

HIGH OFFICIAL: I want war. I want war!

ROIMA: And we want to go back to our homes and live in peace. (*To the crowd*) Go back, go back, this is not our place.

(*The crowd silently disperses.*)

LIGHTS CHANGE

Closure

A CROWD, *composed of the cast members, gather on stage and sing "Wild Dogs." A wire barricade encloses the SLUM and separates the* HIGH OFFICIAL *and his colleagues from the rest. Together they sing "Wild Dogs."*

CROWD: *We are wild dogs*
Shit and gold's our food.
We can't live off pity
Happiness must be stolen
With our minds
With our hands
With force
Or in misery we'll remain.

We are wild dogs
Ready to fight if need be.
Money doesn't fall from the sky
And prayer is often useless.
Where is there honor?
It comes from power and wealth!
Embrace them, embrace them.
Or downtrodden we'll remain
Or downtrodden we'll remain.

(The crowd disbands, splitting apart, to return to the place from where they came, that dank wet underground world without hope.)

LIGHTS DIE

THE END

III

Julini's Opera

Translated by John H McGlynn

Main Characters

JULINI, a transsexual, Roima's deceased girlfriend
ROIMA, a gang leader (with Tibal)
TIBAL, a gang leader (with Roima)
TUMINAH, Tibal's sister, a former prostitute, and Roima's current lover
GUIDE, Julini's guide in the afterlife
OFFICIAL, a high government official
THE WIFE, spouse of the high government official
P.A./PAIJO, the high government official's personal assistant

Other Characters

BILUN, a fabulist (in team with Sawil)
BONAR, a brothel guard
DOCTOR, a doctor to the high government official
DUING, a transsexual, Tuminah's personal assistant
KASIJAH, a deceased prostitute
KUMIS, deceased gang leader
MADAM, manager of the gang-owned brothel
MINISTER, a government official, the Minister of Home Affairs
SAWIL, a fabulist (in team with Bilun)
TARSIH, former brothel manager, now deceased
VOICE, the voice of an unseen police officer

+

Transsexuals: ESYI, IKE (pronounced "Ick-uh"), LAILA, SYENI, TÉA,
WANDA
Gang Members: BAJENET, BLEKI
Prostitutes: ADÉ, ANTJE (pronounced "Ahn-chuh"), DEWI, EVA, SRI
Policemen: POLICE 1, POLICE 2, POLICE 3
Watchmen: WATCHMAN 1, WATCHMAN 2
Heavenly Guards: GUARD 1, GUARD 2

Production History

Julini's Opera was first staged by Teater Koma at the Jakarta Arts Center, Taman Ismail Marzuki, in November 1986. The play was first published in Indonesian that same year.

Introductory Scene

A theater. Nighttime. There is revelry everywhere with much noise and music, a nearly cacophonous sound. The smell of food, perfume, and incense linger in the air. Festive but simultaneously claustrophobic.

A group of musicians is playing old swing and jazz songs. A raucous crowd surrounds them. The sounds of a trumpet, a drum, a cello, timpani and clarinet play fill the air.

It is 7:30 PM. Flashes of various colored light, like laser beams, cut through the sky. The music grows louder, more insistent, resembling the sound of a million cockroaches flapping their wings simultaneously as if preparing to do something— possibly attack—or that of a million bumblebee swarming in a tree.

At 7:45 PM the music grows louder with a deeper undercurrent. The musicians are swept away by their own songs. The music is off key but arresting, mysterious. There are two sources of musical sounds. One without musicians, from underground. The other from the musicians, which is off key.

At 8:00 PM the music grows louder still. More frightening, More insistent, There is a vengeful tone in the sound.

> *Rise from your long sleep*
> *Rid yourself of dreams and desires*
> *Crawl out from the drain pipes*
> *Fend off shame and abuse*
> *Who can stem the tide*
> *When we cockroaches rise as one?*

1

Early morning, before sunrise, on a Jakarta street that runs through a slum. A GOVERNMENT OFFICIAL *is jogging with* P.A., *his personal assistant, whose name is Paijo. Two police officers in uniform,* POLICE 1 *and* POLICE 2, *accompany them.*

OFFICIAL: What's today's report?

POLICE 1: The city is safe; the situation stable, sir.

POLICE 2: Well, except on the outskirts, sir, where there is growing criminal activity.

      (POLICE 1 *kicks him in the shin.*)

      Ouch!

OFFICIAL: What was that?

POLICE 1: Well, yes, there was a report about a criminal gang planning something, but it's still suspect. Don't worry, sir. Even if the report is true, the situation is under control.

OFFICIAL: Whether it's true or not, criminal gangs make people nervous. Preventative medicine is what's needed. Look into it.

POLICE 2: I'm pretty sure it's something big they're planning, sir.

      (POLICE 1 *kicks* POLICE 2 *again.*)

      Ouch!

OFFICIAL: That makes it even more urgent. They need to be weeded out, down to their roots. If we let them grow strong, they'll take over the place.

      You two can go now. Come back to me when you have a complete and written report. Then I'll take a look at it.

      Go on now. I'm in a private capacity here. I don't need you with me.

POLICE 1:	Yes, sir.

(POLICE 1 *kicks* POLICE 2 *yet again.*)

POLICE 2: Ouch!

POLICE 1: You idiot! You fuck up everything. I say things are stable and you say thing are bad.

(*The* POLICE *leave. The* OFFICIAL *continues his morning run.*)

OFFICIAL: Hey, Paijo, how many K have we run?

P.A.: Ten, sir.

OFFICIAL: What's our target for today?

P.A.: Fifteen, sir

(*They take a left-hand turn off the main road into a narrow and fetid-smelling alleyway.*)

OFFICIAL: (*Confused*) What the...? How did we end up here?

P.A.: I don't know, sir. I just followed when you went to the left, sir. We should have gone straight. What, you're turning again? You should be going straight. If you're going to turn, turn to the right, not the left. Geez, you're still going left. How come you can't go straight?

OFFICIAL: Don't know myself, but so be it. Let's just go where our feet take us. But look at this place. It's a slum. And what's that in front of us?

P.A.: A huge pile of trash, sir.

OFFICIAL: And that over there?

P.A.: A collapsed bridge, sir.

OFFICIAL: And those huts.... Who lives in them?

P.A.: Our poor, sir, most of whom don't have official IDs.

OFFICIAL: What are those children doing, running around without any clothes? Aren't they cold?

P.A.:   When food is hard to come by, clothes are in even more scarce supply.

OFFICIAL: But what are they doing, running around here like that.

P.A.:   It's not that they're running around, sir. This is where they live. Because they don't have homes to live in, this is their home, sir.

OFFICIAL: Beneath the open sky?

P.A.:   Yes, sir.

OFFICIAL: Is this real? Not something some fool playwright made up?

P.A.:   It's real, sir. It's real.

OFFICIAL: Why have I never been seen a report about this?

P.A.:   Well, you'd end up getting angry, sir.

(They continue to jog.)

OFFICIAL: Look at all those Caterpillars and riot police. What's going on, Paijo?

P.A.:   Eviction, sir. This area has been slated for demolition because it's a source of immorality

OFFICIAL: What's the name of this place?

P.A.:   Lokasari, sir.

OFFICIAL: Lokasari? You mean, that prostitution complex? But there was a court case about that and the city lost. So, why is it being torn down?

P.A.:   You must be joking, sir. The city never loses.

OFFICIAL: Tell me, Paijo, who are we, really?

P.A.:   Well, you run the city and I am your personal assistant.

OFFICIAL:	(*Stopping suddenly*) Oh, oh.... What's happening, Paijo? I can't see anything. What's happening? It hurts. I've gone blind!
P.A.:	You're fooling, aren't you sir? You can't go blind from jogging.
OFFICIAL:	I can't see anything. It hurts, Paijo. My eyes hurt. All of a sudden, everything is dark.

LIGHTS CHANGE

2

In the sky somewhere. JULINI *appears dressed in a white wedding dress, followed by a* GUIDE *and a troupe of* MUSICIANS.

JULINI:	We're here? This place? Now what I do?
GUIDE:	Just wait. Stay calm and cool.
JULINI:	How can I be cool in these clothes? I'm hot and uncomfortable. Where are we going, anyway?
GUIDE:	I told you before: to meet your fiancée. (*To the* MUSICIANS) You guys go on ahead. Leave us here. Go on now.
JULINI:	Do we still have far to go?
GUIDE:	Yeah, a bit of a ways.
JULINI:	And that's where Roima is now?
GUIDE:	I can't say. All I know is what I have been assigned to do: to escort you through three gateways of three buildings.
	(*The* MUSICIANS *leave. Gradually the sound of their music grows fainter until it dies altogether.*)

LIGHTS CHANGE

3

Somewhere. Anywhere. Colored lights circle fill the sky. A more sinister kind of music is heard and the sound of a choir gradually blends with this sinister-sounding music.

Members of a criminal gang are practicing pencak silat *moves with* ROIMA *and* TIBAL *in the lead.* TUMINAH *is relaxing while being tended to by* DUING. *There is singing.*

ALL: (*Singing "Roaches"*)

You're a cockroach, we are cockroaches
Roaches sing, roaches howl, roaches roar
They come in waves
You're a cockroach, we are cockroaches
Roaches crawl, scream, roaches slouch
They come with thunder

You're a cockroach, we are cockroaches
Roaches crack when stepped on
Roaches demand, roaches shit
Roaches strike, break apart, destroy
Roaches devour, make everything their prey
Roaches panic, roaches shriek, confused
Distressed, depressed

If everyone were roaches
With whom could one pick a fight?
There is only a roach on the throne
With anger in his eyes and a scowl on his lips
"Uphold justice! Long live democracy!"

You're a roach, we are roaches, you're a roach
We are roaches, you're a roach, we are roaches

LIGHTS CHANGE

4

Morning. The home of the OFFICIAL. *The* OFFICIAL *is seated, his eyes still hurting him. His* P.A., *is with him as is his* WIFE, *who is angry with him.*

WIFE: When you're sick and need something, that's when you come whining to me. But when you're out having fun, where am I to be?

OFFICIAL: I'm in pain. I don't know why but my eyes suddenly hurt. All I'm asking is for help. Can you get a compress for my eyes? Maybe that will make it better.

WIFE: Get your own compress, or maybe ask Tuminah for help.

OFFICIAL: How can you bring up her name again?! That was ten years ago. I admitted my mistake and changed my ways. You know how men are; they stray sometimes. And it was only for a little while and I told you I was sorry. But now my eyes, my eyes are hurting me.

WIFE: Have you really forgotten her?

OFFICIAL: I swear. I swear I've forgotten her.

WIFE: (*Erupting with anger*) How can I believe you? Look at this photograph! Who's in it? You and Tuminah in each other's arms. And look at what's written on the back. Go ahead, read it!

OFFICIAL: I can't read it. I can't even see.

WIFE: "For my beloved Tuminah, from your man." And then, there it is, your million-dollar signature on the photograph for that slut. Don't you dare deny it. I found the photo in one of your books. And you're telling me now that you've forgotten that whore?

OFFICIAL: My God, when was that photo taken? Even I had forgotten about that. What's important is that you know I've forgotten her. If you want to tear it up, go ahead!

WIFE: Do that yourself!

OFFICIAL: Here! Give it to me.

(She hands him the photograph and he tears it up.)

Satisfied now!? Oh, my eyes, my eyes.

LIGHTS CHANGE

5

Morning. Near the home of the OFFICIAL.

Night. At the headquarters of ROIMA *and* TIBAL.

JULINI *and the* GUIDE *observe what is happening.*

JULINI: Wow! This is just like watching television!

GUIDE: Yeah, like a scene in a soap opera. Let's see what those gangsters are up to. It's night time there at their headquarters.

(The chorus slowly fades. ROIMA *then begins to speak.)*

ROIMA: Welcome, welcome.... Thank you one and all for your presence here. For those of you not from Jakarta, you might be surprised by the wretched state of this place, our headquarters, but we are leaving it just as it is.

Bit by bit, we're getting richer, and we have branches now, not just here in the capital; We have them throughout the entire archipelago. But it was from this kind of place where we began, so we must never forget it. In fact, we must preserve it so that we will always remember our past and will always be cautious and humble.

Another thing to remember is "exercise." For anyone living beneath the tip of a dagger, physical exercise is a must. That's why I asked that you come here, not in suits and ties, but in *pencak silat* attire. We call this "simplicity."

TIBAL: (*Spitting*) Bah!

ROIMA: Our aim is to become, not just a group of thugs who know only how to fight, but a strong and efficient organization with enough financial backing to control the economy of this country. This is something I'm sure we can do and this is my promise to you: that there will come a day when all of you will become men of means, respected people, no longer cockroaches who crawl beneath other people's feet.

BAJENET: Boss, you sure can talk the talk. Ever since the days of Mas Kumis, we've always been the underdogs, the losers.

(TIBAL *growls.* ROIMA *notices and looks at him askance. Meanwhile,* TUMINAH *is having her nails done by* DUING *who is applying colored polish to them.*)

TIBAL: Losers? (*Growling again*) Always losers? Maybe we are the underclass, the roaches, but we can't give up. It's time that we rose up and showed people who we are. It was from Kumis, your former leader, who is now dead and in the grave, that you got your timidity—always moving around in the dark, and then scampering away when your work is done. But I and Roima want you to have souls of lions. Of tigers. To be men! Nobody is allowed to give up, least not without a fight. You can't be like Bleki here...

BLEKI: Yes, *Bang?*

TIBAL: Yes, Bleki here, whom I have taken underwing precisely because of his dog-like attitude.

BLEKI: Yes, *Bang...*

TIBAL:	Willing to work for anyone as long as his life is safe. Isn't that right, Bleki?
BLEKI:	Yes, *Bang.*
TIBAL:	Kick him, cuss him, spit on him, he doesn't care, not if his boss is doing it. No sense of self-respect. Isn't that right, Bleki?
BLEKI:	That's right, *Bang.*
TUMINAH:	Duing?
DUING:	Yes, Tuminah dahling?
TUMINAH:	Pay attention to what you're doing. Are you painting my fingers or my nails?
DUING:	Your fingers, Tuminah, oh, I mean your nails.
TUMINAH:	Idiot. Clean that polish off my fingers.
DUING:	Right away, Tuminah.

(JULINI *jumps around ecstatically.*)

JULINI:	Hey, I know those people! My word! That's Tibal, Tuminah, and Roima.... Roima, my husband, my idol, the love of my life.
GUIDE:	No use trying to approach them. They won't be able to see you. You have no contact with them. Their world and your world are different now.
JULINI:	Come on! How could Roima not know me? I don't believe you.
GUIDE:	Have you forgotten? You're dead!
JULINI:	How can dead people talk? Roima! What, he's laughing... (*The* GANG MEMBERS *start laughing when seeing* TIBAL *ride* BLEKI *like a horse.*)

TIBAL: Sometimes it's hard to decide whether this creature here is a person or an animal.

ROIMA: You're going too far, Tibal. Bleki gave himself up to us. For that, he should be treated well.

TIBAL: I agree. And I think that we do treat Bleki well. Just ask him. Hey, Bleki, speaking as your superior, am I good or bad?

BLEKI: You're good, *Bang*.

TIBAL: Are you happy or not?

BLEKI: I'm happy, Bang. Do you want to play horse again?

(*The* GANG *laughs.*)

TIBAL: You see, Bleki doesn't object.

ROIMA: Enough of this. To save time, I'd like to explain the reason for this meeting.

JULINI: Oh, Roima.... My heart flitters just to see you.

He's even better looking now—so tall, so lean, and that moustache of his.... A real toned dish!

GUIDE: "Toned dish?" You mean "Adonis"?

JULINI: Whatever...

GUIDE: Julini, we must be on our way. Don't bother them.

(JULINI *ignores the* GUIDE *and descends directly into the middle of the group.*)

ROIMA: We're planning something big and if it works out, we'll make out many times over. But you, as branch leaders, must keep our plans secret. If there is any leak, we're all dead.

(*As if being bothered by a mosquito,* ROIMA *swats the air with his hands.*)

JULINI: Roima.... Roima honey...

ROIMA: (*Still slapping the air with his hands*) We'll call in outside experts and study from them.

JULINI: (*Annoyed, shrieking*) Roima! What are you doing, pretending not to know me? It's me, Roima, Julini!

ROIMA: (*Irritated*) Damn mosquito! And a big one, too. Die, damn you!

            (ROIMA *opens an assignment book.*)

JULINI: (*Downcast*) He thinks I'm a mosquito. He really doesn't know me.

GUIDE: (*Laughing*) I told you, he can't see you. Your world and his world are different now.

JULINI: And Tuminah, too? (*To* TUMINAH) Tuminah, it's me, Julini. You can see me, can't you? Your eyes are open and I'm a million times bigger than a mosquito. You must be able to see me.

TUMINAH: (*Screaming*) Duing!

DUING: Yes, Tuminah? What is it?

TUMINAH: There's a mosquito. Get the bug spray.

DUING: Ok, ok.... There, I see it and it's a big one too. A male one, too. Ouch, it bit me. It really is a male. (*Spraying*) Die you fucker.

JULINI: They think I'm a male mosquito. This is just way too much.

GUIDE: It's called reality, Julini.

JULINI: Then why did I have to dress up like this? I look like a giant puppet. I was told that I was going to greet my fiancée.

Well that's my husband, Roima, and there's no man I love other man than him. (*Singing*)

There are many handsome men
But he is the one I most love
For years, both days and nights
Only his image I dreamed of
Roima, Roima, oh, Roima
A manly man, a manly man
My handsome husband, my beloved one

So, if Roima can't see me, who is this supposed fiancée? I've had no other man in my life.

GUIDE: Oh, really?

JULINI: Well, I know there were others but that was when I was working as an escort.

GUIDE: You, an escort?

JULINI: Well, that's the polite word anyway. A he-whore is what some people called me—even though I'm a woman, a true woman.

Sure, there have been many men who have laid their heads on my breast. But they were just customers. I was with them only for the money, not because of love. It's only Roima I love. It's like the saying, "once free, forever free." Once Roima, forever Roima.

The world turns dark when he's not in it. It would be better for me not to be able to see him than the other way around. Is this an illusion?

GUIDE: No, it's reality. You're dead, Julini. Don't forget.

JULINI: You're wrong. This is a play. A joke. Who can prove that I am dead? Everyone can see me. Isn't that right? This is a play, right?

GUIDE: Yes, it's a play. But in this play, in its reality, you're dead. Can't you get that through your head?

JULINI: I won't have it. I won't! Who wrote this play anyway? Who?! Come on up here so that I can ask you straight to your face why you made me one of the walking dead.

GUIDE: It's pointless to ask such a question. No one can answer it. Even the playwright's confused.

JULINI: Well then he should leave me out of this altogether. It's not fair. He's confused but has me dancing from the end of his strings? I was dead and at peace and now he brings me back to life. What? Doesn't he have something better to do?

              (ROIMA *finishes checking his assignment book.*)

ROIMA: Hey, Bajenet.

BAJENET: Yes, boss.

ROIMA: How did your investigation of the banks in the Sudirman and Kuningan areas go?

BAJENET: That's what I wanted to tell you. They're all using high-tech security devices. Really high-tech. For little fish like us...

TIBAL: (*Shouting*) Hey! We are not little fish. We're the best in the world at what we do so don't belittle us. You can get an inferiority complex from thinking that way. I don't like it. We're the best in the world. Got it?!

BAJENET: Alright, boss! But for the best in the world gang like ours, we still don't have the technology that they do. It's all foreign stuff, imported gadgets. Just one tiny wrong move and it's tweet! They got lasers, CCTV, alarms. Do you think we can outsmart equipment like that?

ROIMA: So what do you suggest?

BAJENET: I think it would be better to keep things just as they are. Keep things small. There's no stress that way. We're robbers, not salesmen, after all.

(*Suddenly a* GANG MEMBER *enters, out of breath.*)

What is it?

GANG MEMBER: There's robbers coming this way. Robbers!

TIBAL: Well so fucking what?

ROIMA: What are you trying to say?

BANDIT: Sorry, sorry, I meant "police". There are lots of them out there and they are coming this way.

(*The* GANG MEMBERS *panic.*)

TIBAL: (*Screaming angrily*) Who squealed? Son-of-a-bitch! (*Angrily*) How did they find this place?

ROIMA: Calm down. We'll break up. Don't go in groups. Everyone goes his separate way. We'll meet a week from now at Safe house Number 3 at twelve midnight. Now scram.

(*The* GANG MEMBERS *hurry to leave.*)

Tibal, we need to look into this.

TUMINAH: Duing...

DUING: Yes, Tuminah dahling?

TUMINAH: Don't forget my beauty case.

DUING: I won't, but, could I ask you a favor?

TUMINAH: What?

DUING: Will you not call me "Duing." That was my old name but now I'm Inge. I had a proper name-change ceremony and everything.

TUMINAH: OK, but not now. There's no time for that.

DUING: (*Disappointed*) OK, Tuminah.

TUMINAH: What's in your head? You can change your name all you like but for me you're still going to be Duing, shoeshine boy from Kalipasir. Now let's go.

(*The two leave quickly.*)

JULINI: Roima.... (*Sadly*) They're all leaving. So what about me?

(*The GUIDE laughs and begins to sing "Julini's Tale" with JULINI later joining in.*)

GUIDE: *Oh, that poor transsexual*
            Known by the name of Julini
            Who once worked as a masseuse
            But gave little extras on the side
            On the night of a full moon
            She was struck by stray bullets
            In her chest and bellybutton
            And died in her boyfriend's arms

JULINI: *People say that I am dead*
            Who knows what to believe
            Proof and facts are strange
            In fact I felt nothing at all
            It was like waking from a long sleep
            My body was as light as cotton
            Which the wind then carried away

GUIDE: *A lucky transsexual was she*
            A monument was erected in her name
            A statue where people pay their respects
            In life she was a model transsexual
            Never once going through rehabilitation

JULINI:

What's the meaning of a monument
I would much prefer to be alive
But the worst of it, the worst is
People prefer mute statues
Who silently stare, make no demands
In fact they hate flesh and blood
Those irritants full of demands

(*Screaming angrily*)

But I am flesh and blood! People say I'm dead, but I am still flesh and blood with feelings and demands.

(*A phalanx of* POLICEMEN *enter with* POLICE 1 *and* POLICE 2 *in the lead.*)

POLICE 1:

Here, did you say?

POLICE 2:

Yes. (*To the other* POLICEMEN) Now spread out! Check every corner!

POLICE 3:

Yes, sir!

(*The* POLICEMEN *spread out, searching the area for* GANG MEMBERS.)

POLICE 2:

The meeting was supposed to be here. That's what our informant said.

POLICE 1:

How likely is that? Kumis has been dead for a long time. His gang scattered and they don't have power anymore. I think someone was feeding you a line. Tell your informant to check again.

POLICE 2:

I'll do that but let's wait and see. The report was clear: that Kumis's gang has reformed and is getting back their strength. In fact, I was told, they're now getting support from abroad.

POLICE 1:   That's bullshit. Did you see the news on television last night? It was announced that the city is completely safe, 100% safe. They wouldn't lie, would they? Everything is stable and under control.

And what's that crap about getting help from abroad? (*Laughing*) Do you think gangsters here know how to speak English? How are they going to communicate? Tarzan language? In the criminal world, communication is the most important thing.

POLICE 2:   Maybe you are right...

(*Having finished searching the area, the other* POLICEMEN *return.*)

POLICE 1:   So?

POLICE 3:   It's safe, chief. No sign of things out of the ordinary.

POLICE 1:   What a waste of time. Alright then, break up and return to headquarters.

POLICE 2 and 3: Yes, sir.

(*The* POLICEMEN *are suddenly surprised when two men in astronaut suits appear. These two men,* SAWIL *and* BILUN *are known as fabulists.*)

SAWIL: An island. Let's say we buy an uninhabited island for US$ 7 billion and then plant trees on it. How long would it take for the trees to mature?

BILUN: Eight years, maybe.

SAWIL: OK, eight years. So let's count. What would be the price of saplings?

BILUN: A hundred maybe?

SAWIL: A hundred what? Dollars?

BILUN: Rupiah.

SAWIL: I'm sure that's too low in rupiah but in dollars too high. Let's say twenty dollars. If we buy 10,000 saplings then 10,000 times 20 is 200,000 dollars. Plywood is expensive, right?

BILUN: Well the market is on the rise, least that's what I read in the paper.

SAWIL: Exactly. Our business would be a sure bet. Where's that calculator? Let's figure out just exactly how much we could make. How many sheets of plywood can you get from one tree?

          (*The* POLICEMEN, *who had been watching and saying nothing, now decide to act.*)

POLICE 2:   (*Shouting*) Hands in the air! Put 'em up! Who are you?

SAWIL: Who, us? I'm Sawil and that's Bilun. We're businessmen.

POLICE 2:   Raise your hands higher and don't try anything funny? Keep your hands off that bag. What's in it? A gun?

SAWIL: Go ahead and open it, sir. We're businessmen. Really. I swear.

          (POLICE 1 *inspects the bag and removes from it a jumble of ragged sheets of paper full of incomprehensible markings.*)

POLICE 1:   (*Laughing*) They're loony! Let's let them go.

POLICE 2:   But, sir...

POLICE 1:   Are you really businessmen?

SAWIL: Yes, sir.

BILUN: I swear. We just landed here.... By the way, what's the name of this place, sir?

POLICE 1:   Rawapening. (*Smiling*) And what do you trade in?

SAWIL:	Sometimes, we buy and sell islands. We deal in cruise ships as well. And, when cash is flush, we even deal in planets and planetariums.
	You know that space shuttle that blew up last year? They bought it from us. But the explosion wasn't our fault. Isn't that so, Bilun?
BILUN:	Yeah. We warned them that the thing was old and that it was dangerous but they insisted, so we finally let it go. Sold it at a real low price.
SAWIL:	And that passenger ship that sank four years ago? That came from us too. We told them that it should be used for scrap metal but they bought it anyway. So who's to blame? It wasn't our fault, right?
POLICE 1:	Yeah, yeah. You can go now.
POLICE 2:	(*Still anxious*) Sir...
POLICE 1:	Enough already, they're not dangerous. So, go on now.
SAWIL:	So where were we, Bilun?
BILUN:	One tree would produce how many cubic meters of plywood?
SAWIL:	That's right. Let's figure that out. So how high is the average adult tree?
BILUN:	12 meters.
SAWIL:	OK, 12 meter... but some grow as tall as 40 meters... so...
	(*As* SAWIL *and* BILUN *disappear, their voices fade.*)
POLICE 2:	Why did you let them go, sir?
POLICE 1:	What, you want to arrest two crazy people? We're police, not shrinks. Let's get out of here.

(*The two* POLICE *officers leave.*)

GUIDE: You know those two, don't you?

JULINI: Yeah, but what's the use of calling out to them? They wouldn't be able to see me; they'd think I was a mosquito.

GUIDE: This is good. You're beginning to understand now. Shall we go?

JULINI: Where to?

GUIDE: Just follow me. You'll find out soon enough.

(JULINI *follows the* GUIDE *listlessly as if having no power over her own movement. Soon, they come to a gateway.*)

JULINI: Amazing! What's this?

GUIDE: This is the first gateway, the one to the building called "Nine Lightning Bolts and Seven Suns."

LIGHTS CHANGE

6

Morning. At the home of the government OFFICIAL *whose luxurious furnishings indicate he's a man of great wealth. The* OFFICIAL, *who is moaning because his eyes hurt, is surrounded by his* WIFE, *his* P.A., *and a* DOCTOR.

OFFICIAL: Oh my god, oh my god, it hurts so much.

WIFE: Be calm, dear. The doctor is here to help you.

OFFICIAL: Nobody can help me. My eyes hurt so much.

WIFE: Dear...

DOCTOR: Sir, if you keep moaning, how am I going to find out what's wrong?

WIFE:

I don't understand. My husband has always been in good health. Never any complaint whatsoever. But for five days now he's been screaming because of sore eyes. During the day he can work just fine but in the morning, when coming home from jogging, he's always moaning.

OFFICIAL:

My eyes, my eyes.... Stop your talking and try to find out the reason. Oh, they hurt so much.

DOCTOR:

Eye infections are common but let me have a look to see what we're dealing with.

OFFICIAL:

Even when you speak they hurt. When a person is near me and talking it's like their words are needles being punched into my eyes. Owww!

DOCTOR:

Alright, alright. but try to be calm so that I can take a look.

OFFICIAL:

Fast, do it fast.

(Just as the DOCTOR *puts his hand to the eyes of the* OFFICIAL, *the* OFFICIAL *jumps up and blocks his touch.)*

Don't touch them. They hurt.

WIFE:

Dear, we all know your eyes hurt and that you're in pain but you must let the doctor look at them. You're acting like a child. Here we are trying to help you but you won't let us.

Well then, if that's what you want, so be it. This is ridiculous. The older you are, the more of a model you're supposed to be for others, but you are turning into a joke instead.

What if the people were to know that you, the Director of the 4-H Program, was acting this way? You'd be embarrassed, wouldn't you?

OFFICIAL:

(Finally giving in) Yes, yes, you're right. Go ahead, Doc, and take a look.

DOCTOR: That's better. Now sit back down and relax.

            (*The* DOCTOR *takes out his instruments.*)

OFFICIAL: What are those? They're scary looking.

DOCTOR: Trust me, OK?

            (*The* DOCTOR, *sings the first verse of "The Song of the Official and the Doctor."*)

DOCTOR: *Medical instruments are indeed scary devices*
            But they are only for humanitarian purposes
            The way a doctor inspects a patient
            Often looks like torture
            But it is only for healing purposes

            (*The* OFFICIAL *sings the second verse.*)

OFFICIAL: *Am I in fact ill?*
            My eyes truly do feel to be in pain
            But there is a pain that cannot be seen
            Deep down inside my chest

            (*The* WIFE *and* P.A. *sing backup.*)

WIFE & P.A.: *Curucucu, curucucu, dadida dididi*

DOCTOR: *There are so many kinds of illnesses*
            Each with its own name and cause
            The body and each of the senses
            Are all part of my duties to man
            But as to matters of conscience, who am I to know?

OFFICIAL: *My eyes are the main gateway*
            Of knowing what is good or bad
            So many sights I have seen
            And all have a scary look for me

WIFE & P.A.: *Curucucu, curucucu, dadida dididi*

OFFICIAL: And what have I been doing all this time? I'm busy planning budgets and holding seminars and workshops for a brilliant future. But what have I been doing about the present? It's that question that kept going through my mind, one to which I could find no answer.

And then, all of a sudden, I felt the world go dark. I was blinded by pain and fear. I have been spending all my time in buildings, offices, cars, and hotels. I read about poverty, sure, but have always felt the stories are just a ploy on the part of those who are jealous and envious of me—just overblown news, a tactic to increase their own popularity.

But then, when seeing it with my own eyes, I was instantly blinded from the awareness that I could do nothing because I am not my own person anymore. My hands, my legs, my mouth, are only to be used for the corps. For the party. For tactical purposes. For integrity. For loyalty—mono-loyalty. For my superiors. For so on and so forth.

I am just a puppet. That's what happened and only now I realize it. I am blind because of ignorance. I am blind because I do nothing. It's not my eyes that are infected but my soul and my conscience. And you can't possibly heal me. It hurts, it hurts, owww...

(*He runs away.*)

WIFE: Dear...!

P.A.:   Amazing. That's the best speech I've ever heard him give in thirty years serving the country—and extemporaneous at that!

WIFE: (*Calling to her husband*) Darling, don't leave me. Remember, you are a civil servant, not a poet.

Doctor, please go after him. Take pity on him.

DOCTOR: We'll go after him together.

(*They exit followed by the others.*)

LIGHTS CHANGE

7

Night. At the gang's headquarters. TIBAL *is angry.* ROIMA *is trying to stay calm.* TUMINAH *is unconcerned.* DUING *tails* TUMINAH *like a faithful dog,*

TIBAL: This is fucking unbelievable. A mole in our gang? You're too weak, Roima. It's a cruel and bloody world out there but act like a priest. You need an iron fist to lead a gang.

ROIMA: Sure, you need an iron hand but that doesn't mean you should be high-handed.

TIBAL: They need to fear us. We got control of the gang through blood and it's only with blood we'll keep them under our command. Your plan is too complicated.

ROIMA: What do you mean?

TIBAL: We have to put our plan into action now. Straightway with no twists. Power is power. And the one who has it is in control. We only need the help of the others to take us to the top of the power chain.

ROIMA: Tibal, it's that need for revenge you felt in the past that still controls you. Kumis messed up your future and so you killed him. I know that, but now you're going to mess up the future of others. You act too quickly; you don't use your brain.

TIBAL: Don't talk to me like that. I got a brain and I use it. I just want to see our plan put into action soon.

ROIMA: But that's where you're wrong. My plan needs time. It won't happen overnight. Power is control, I know that, but how do you get control? Through money! Lots of it...! Which is what I'm working on.

            We have casinos, whorehouses, movie theaters, and hotels. Sure, with the money we're making, we could all be living large. But I'm waiting, holding back. Besides, I don't like being wasteful.

TUMINAH: Hey, Roima, if you have something to say, say it. Don't beat around the bush. Don't you think I don't know what you're getting at? Who you're talking about?

ROIMA: I'm not talking about anyone.

TUMINAH: You're talking about me. And yes, maybe I do like to spend money. Maybe I do like nice jewelry and living the good life. That's what you're trying to say, isn't it?

ROIMA: That's not what I meant.

TUMINAH: Seems to me that's what you're talking about. Well, OK.... (*Shouting at* DUING) You need to get out of my hair. Remove that nail polish. Can't you see I'm talking serious here.

DUING: Alright, Tuminah.

TUMINAH: So I want to live a happy life, is that wrong? To enjoy the things we own, is that wrong? Ten years I worked as a prostitute—Not a great experience!—and now that we have some money, we're supposed to keep living in hell? What are savings for? Who is supposed to benefit from them? I eat from the profit in my hand; I don't hope for what's in dreams. Is that wrong?

I don't care how you get your power or money. The point is, I'm not bothering you. I'm just taking my fair share. Better you speak straight than insinuate. Maybe ask yourself what you're working so hard for.

ROIMA: (*Angry*) Why? Don't you don't know what you worked hard for?

TUMINAH: Do you? And who cares anyway?

ROIMA: I know what I'm working for. Only horses and buffaloes work hard without knowing what they're working for. We have money now. We're rich. But do we have respect?

TUMINAH: Is that what you want? Respect?

ROIMA: I'm not finished speaking. We're low class because we earn our fare with fists and daggers. But those two things: respect, and honor. Even for people like us who live in the gutters, honor and respect are important. Aren't they?

TIBAL: Enough already...

ROIMA: Wouldn't you someday like to be able to mix with the suit-and-tie class and talk about golf, paintings, and the fall in the price of oil on the world market? I do. I want that. I want to be able to sit at the same dining table with that class of people and able to discuss things without stuttering and embarrassment.

And that's the direction we're moving in now! Is it wrong to study, to learn? We may be stupid but we now have the chance to change things. That's a chance you can't waste. We have the money we need as capital. I don't want to be a pack horse forever. We have to be bosses.

TIBAL: Enough already. Enough...

ROIMA: We're always doing things on the sly. We have to pay people to do things for us because we know that as soon as we show our faces, the police will drag us in.

I don't want to be behind the screen. I want people to know who I am—the brains behind the operation. I don't want to hide and be on the run my entire life.

TIBAL: Enough, Roima! Can't you just shut up for once.

ROIMA: You've changed, Tuminah. You're not the Tuminah I once knew. You're too easily satisfied. Like a candle whose flame has been snuffed out. A pack horse. (*Exiting sadly.*)

TUMINAH: (*Crying*) What's happening? Why has it come to this?

TIBAL: He has too much ambition. He wants to be respectable. (*Spitting*) Wants to open a bank. Maybe he does have talent. Maybe he is smart guy, but he's going too fast and that makes him dangerous. (*Exits.*)

TUMINAH: (*While crying*) He's taken to yelling at me.... Tell me, Duing, have I changed?

DUING: Changed? Of course you've changed. You have bigger necklaces, rings, gem-covered bracelets, and diamond-studded hair clips.

TUMINAH: I don't mean that, you idiot. I mean "me," without the necklaces and jewelry. Me, just me, stripped down to my naked self.

DUING: No! Don't get naked. I wouldn't like the comparison. Don't take what Roima said to heart. He's just upset is all.

TUMINAH: He doesn't love me anymore.

DUING: He still loves you, Tuminah. I swear. Sometimes, when I'm massaging him, he'll say, "No matter what, Duing, Tuminah is an extraordinary woman, even if all she does is eat, sleep, and wear fancy clothes..."

TUMINAH: Did he really say that, Duing? Did he?

DUING: Uhm, uhm, no, it wasn't him. I just...

TUMINAH: Come here. I want to slap your face.

DUING: (*Afraid*) Don't do that!

TUMINAH: (*Screaming*) Come here, you idiot.

DUING: One cheek or two?

TUMINAH: Both of them, toadstool.

             (TUMINAH *slaps* DUING'*s cheeks.*)

DUING: Ow, ow.... You didn't have to slap me three times.

TUMINAH: (*Regaining herself but then crying again*) I know it's true, Duing. Roima doesn't love me anymore. He still has Julini on his mind. It hurts, Duing. Everything I do is to make him like me but he doesn't realize it.

DUING: You have to be patient. Love requires sacrifice.

TUMINAH: I don't need all this; I only need Roima. He should know that. I'm just stupid is all, never even graduated from grade school, but I love him just the same.

             (*She sings "Tuminah's Love"*)

             Love is like a shattering of glass
             Tearing the chest, leaving deep wounds
             Love is like chasing shadows
             Forever and always escaping your grasp

             I am the sky
             You are the sun
             I am the stars
             You are their light

             But now where is the sun
             And where is the light
             Now there's only uncertainty. Uncertainty
             Ohh, this fate of mine.

DUING: There's a saying that there are two ways of getting a man: through food or passion. Look at yourself, Tuminah. You're still fine looking. You should have no trouble getting Roima's back in your arms.

TUMINAH: What do you think all this jewelry and makeup are for? They're for Roima. But you know, Duing, for almost a year now, Roima has not been that way with me. I don't know why. I thought at first he might have another girlfriend but now I don't think that's true. I don't know what to think. Maybe I'm just not attractive anymore.

DUING: You're still good-looking, Tuminah, a true hottie, so please stop your pouting.

TUMINAH: (*Crying*) After he left Julini for me, she was killed and her death haunts him to this day. I think he feels guilty, that it was his fault Julini died. Or maybe he blames me for Julini's death...

DUING: I do have to say, Roima and Julini were quite the couple. Who doesn't know their love story? It's the stuff of legend. And Julini is every trans' idol. It's no surprise a monument was erected in her name.

TUMINAH: (*Erupting with jealousy*) Damn it to hell. What are we talking about this for? What's the use? To Roima, I'm just a piece of shit, a dead candle, garbage.

DUING: Tuminah, oh, Tuminah...

TUMINAH: (*Crying*) And he called me a pack horse.... Fuck! (*Exits.*)

DUING: Wait, Tuminah, wait...!

(TUMINAH *suddenly reappears.*)

TUMINAH: Don't forget my makeup bag.

DUING: Yes, dahling.

LIGHTS CHANGE

8

Nighttime at Julini Plaza, the hangout of the city's transsexual community. JULINI and the GUIDE *appear in another dimension.*

GUIDE: Here we are at the gateway to the second building. This one is called "One Thousand Lightning Bolts and Three Suns."

JULINI: Are we going to go in?

GUIDE: Yes, we are.

JULINI: Is Roima in there?

GUIDE: I can't say. Let's go in and see.

(They go through the gateway.)

JULINI: It looks just the same, both inside and out. No difference at all.

GUIDE: Yes, that is what it looks like. Let's rest a bit.

(Lively music is heard.)

JULINI: What's that?

GUIDE: Friends of yours in another world. You can look but cannot touch.

JULINI: It's like we're invisible, is it? Now you see us, now you don't!

(A group of trans women are singing, dancing, and having a good time. They sing "The Song of Three Pleasures.")

TRANSWOMEN: *What is it that they are looking for?*
Three kinds of pleasures, my love, three:
Pleasures of the body, the mouth, and mind
All three are important and needed

But in order to have them—
These three kinds of pleasures, my love —
A person needs money, hard cash

Nothing in this world is for free
What we can sell, we sell
All that we do, we do to live
Fate is in our own hands
Who else will care? Who else?

(*Suddenly, screams are heard. Two of the trans women, LAILA and TÉA, have begun to fight. The plaza is now scene of commotion.*)

IKE: What's going on with those two?

ESYI: They're fighting over a bottle, I'd guess.

LAILA: (*While entering*) Don't you call me crazy. I know what you're up to. Everyone knows that Bob is my boy. I paid his way here from the village and spruced him up. Now that he's hot, you can't get your hands off him. Respect the rules, OK!?

TÉA: (*While entering*) You're full of it. It's you who can't watch your man. He's the one who started it. I was taking a bath at the well and he rubbed up next to me.

LAILA: And you wanted that, didn't you?

TÉA: I didn't want that. That moustache of his; I don't like it. It tickles. He's not my type I tell you; he's the one who forced himself on me.

LAILA: And you let him!?

TÉA: I was forced. Then, after a while, I just kind of forgot myself?

LAILA: So the truth comes out. You are after Bob.

TÉA: That's a lie. I could get a thousand guys like Bob in a day if I wanted to. What, do you think he's the one and only man in the world? You're the crazy one.

LAILA:	So, you not only insult me, you insult Bob, too. Maybe you do have that sugar daddy, Tibum, behind you but I'm not afraid of you.
TÉA:	What are you bringing Tibum into this? If you want to fight, I'll fight. What can you do anyway? Karate?
	(TÉA *takes a fighting position.*)
LAILA:	You really do want to fight?! Well, OK! (*Doing a kung-fu move*) Hiyah!
TÉA:	(*Dodging the move*) Aha! Missed me!
	(*The group splits into two, one in support of* LAILA, *the other rooting for* TÉA.)
IKE:	Hmm, they're equal at this. (*Calling out*) Come on, Laila, use your inner strength!
ESYI:	Go for her, Téa. You're the champ.
	(TÉA *and* LAILA *continue to fight but neither gets the upper edge. Some of the trans women are placing bets.*)
TÉA:	Hiyah!
LAILA:	You can't touch me!
IKE:	Come on, fight harder!
	(*In the end,* LAILA *and* TÉA *start pulling at each other's hair and the plaza grows even noisier. Suddenly, a siren is heard, causing* TÉA *and* LAILA *to stop fighting. The trans women look around in confusion. A* VOICE *from a battery operated microphone is heard.*)
VOICE:	Attention, attention! Everyone calm down.
IKE:	It's a raid! Run!
	(*Everyone is confused. No one knows what to do.*)

VOICE: It's useless to run! The area is surrounded. Calm down and keep your order. Nothing will happen if you keep your order.

ESYI: (*Weakly*) Oh, Mommy, Mommy, I want to die...

SYENI: What is it, Esy?

ESYI: I wet myself.

VOICE: Who's the leader here?

LAILA: We don't have a leader, sir. We are independent but responsible people, sir, just like that newspaper slogan!

IKE: We're democratic, sir. We are our own leaders.

VOICE: Democratic? No wonder you make such a racket. But OK, who then will be your spokesperson?

            (*They all push one another forward but no one wants to take the lead role. In the end, they all agree that* IKE *should be the spokesperson.*)

VOICE: (*To* IKE) So, you're the spokesperson?

IKE: No choice. You saw it yourself. It was either that or get trampled on by those trannies.

VOICE: Aren't you a tranny too?

IKE: No, sir. I'm a real woman. I just haven't had my operation yet. By the way, who am I talking to anyway? Could you show your face, please.

VOICE: I don't need to show my face. I'm an officer and officers everywhere look just the same. What's your name?

IKE: On my ID card, it says my name is Harun Bawazir Al Kohar Ali Mukadimah Al Khatam bin Nyoo Kam Wong, residing at Kelinci Lane in the 11th subward of the 8th ward. Third of nine children, the only male, born in Tangerang

	25 years ago, whose hobbies are plucking daisy petals and soccer. My uncle is a dentist and my aunt is a film star. We have a car dealer in the family as well. As for me, besides working as a wedding makeup artist...
VOICE:	Stop,stop! Too much information!
IKE:	Well. I just want it to be complete.
VOICE:	Short answers will be sufficient; only what I need to know.
IKE:	Alright.
VOICE:	How many trannies hang out here?
IKE:	Lots.
VOICE:	How many?
IKE:	Haven't done a census.
VOICE:	Do you know the name "Kumis"?
TÉA:	Oh, Kumis, we know. He used to be the strong man around here. But he's dead now. Tibal killed him. Why? Did he come back to life?
VOICE:	That is being looked into.... Were any of you here members of his gang? (*Silence*) If you don't answer I'll have your hair cut off. Answer me now! Were any of you members of Kumis's gang?
TRANSWOMEN:	(*In unison*) No...!
VOICE:	You're lying. (*Silence*) Doesn't matter, we'll find out. We have records on all of you. And whoever turns out to have been in Kumis's gang is not going to escape a sentence.
ESYI:	Oh, Mommy, I want to die.
VOICE:	What's with her?
SYENI:	She wet herself, sir. But Esyi is always that way. Say something, Esyi!

ESYI: I'm afraid...

VOICE: Enough. Why were you fighting earlier? (*Silence*) What was that fight about? Come on, spokesperson, give me an answer.

IKE: Am I still the spokesperson?

VOICE: Yes, you are. So why was there a fight?

IKE: The usual thing, sir. Whenever there's a fight and it's usually about a bottle.

VOICE: They were fighting over a bottle?

IKE: As if you don't know what I'm talking about.... A living bottle that's nice too use and lasts a long time. That's what the fights are usually about. But they usually end quickly and peace returns. We are ladies, after all.

TÉA: Oh, Laila, forgive me, will you?

LAILA: Of course I forgive you, Téa. We're in this thing together, sharing the same fate. And if they throw us in jail, I hope we share the same bed.

TÉA: Oh, Laila...

LAILA: Oh, Téa...

          (*The two embrace and cry.*)

IKE: See what I mean. It's like a play.

VOICE: But you're disturbing the peace. This place isn't safe anymore. You're an embarrassment to the city. Every day, another fight. There's no order around here.

SYENI: It's a market, sir. How's there going to be order? Everyone wants to sell their goods.

LAILA: Yes, this is free trade, free competition.

VOICE: How many times have we had to drag you in but you still keep coming back to this place.

IKE: Well, where else are we going to go, sir?

VOICE: Find another path, the right path.

TÉA: We all want normal lives, sir, but tell us how? Point out the proper way. Don't just drag us in and lock us up.

LAILA: That's right. At least we're not hypocrites. We operate openly yet we are hunted down. Think about it. All those high government officials; they are basically the same but they are given status and rank. Why's that, sir?

VOICE: They get their positions because they have gone through the proper training courses. You haven't. All you do is make a disturbance.

IKE: Well, if a training course will get us a better position, then we're all in for it.

VOICE: Which is exactly why I am here tonight. All of you are to go through a basic 4-H course which, in turn, will lead to other training courses until, in the end, you are good people and good citizens.

SYENI: What does "4-H" stand for, sir?

VOICE: It stands for "head, heart, health, and hands." To use your brain for once; to learn by heart what is right; to keep your disease from spreading; and to keep your hands off others.

SYENI: Long live 4-H!

VOICE: Enough of this now. Now I want you to all line up in a neat and single file, starting with the spokesperson. The others follow behind, one by one. Quickly now. Walk to the vehicle that's already been provided. Begin...

(Together, the TRANSWOMEN *sing "The Song of a Prospective Person.")*

ALL: *In one long line we march forward*
Our path leads to an incredible door
We let ourselves be taken by the course
And enter a human printing machine

Without the knife of ideology
We are not full-fledged humans
Formless clumps of clay to be molded
At the command of the king cockroach

We enter a gigantic machine
To emerge as small machines
After which we can only hope
For a better and brilliant future

Huhuhuuu, daidadududu
Huhuhuu, daridadududu
After that, who in fact are we?
I'm sorry but no one even knows

The machines wheels devour us
Grinds away all conscience and feeling
Turns us into circles, squares or triangles
Whatever shape, just as long as it's the same

That is the meaning of training
Creating a road leading straight ahead
Erecting walls on the right and left
On the way to an ideal form
But where is it that we are going?
Is it to heaven or to hell?

(In a line they all leave the plaza to go to the large vehicle that is waiting for them.)

JULINI: Let's hope for a better future for them.

GUIDE: Yes, indeed.

JULINI: And what about me?

GUIDE: For you the journey is over.

JULINI: What are you talking about? If it were over we would have arrived. But here we are, not knowing where we're going, not knowing how long it will take, who we are going to meet, whether we will be happy or sad.... And you say it's over?

Take pity on the audience who have been waiting ever since the beginning of this play to find out what happens. A dead person coming back to life is something special. They are sure to be expecting something special to happen. Don't you think?

All this time, I've been told to be a spectator. When do I get a chance to perform?

GUIDE: All in due time—at the third gateway.

JULINI: And then?

GUIDE: I can't say yet.

JULINI: Are you a real guide or just a fake. If all you can say is "I can't say," well then, what can you say? What if something were to happen to me? Well, then you'd be sorry.... But you know, the longer we're together like this, the cuter you become, what with your suit and tie, your hair so neatly combed, and your cologne...

GUIDE: Time to get a move on.

JULINI: But wait, look at the statue. It's me, isn't it?

GUIDE: Yes, that's you.

JULINI: Not as good-looking as the original, though! And her breasts, all bare like that...! She could get a cold. And she's holding a banana?! Who is it that made this statue.

SOMEONE: Idries Pulungan.

JULINI: He must like bananas too!

GUIDE: Come on. Do you want to stay here or go?

JULINI: OK, let's go.

(They exit.)

LIGHTS CHANGE

9

Nighttime at the labor supply office for the brothel TIBAL *and* ROIMA *plan to open.* TUMINAH *and* BAJENET *are there along with three prospective* CANDIDATES *who are demonstrating their singing skills. They sing "The Mare's Song."*

CANDIDATES: *I fly with your hand on the control*
    Take me to wherever you wish to go
    For I am just your riding horse

    You and I are two fiery horses
    Flying high, cutting through the sky
    Reaching the peak of unmatched pleasure

    Do not speak of love in this place
    Love is nothing but an empty promise
    You and I are two figures who are now one

    Take me wherever you want to go
    Because your hand is on the reigns
    And I am only a riding horse

    (After the song, they wait to be called.)

TUMINAH: What do you think, Bajenet?

BAJENET: With their talent, how can we turn them down? They can do two jobs: sing and that other thing. It's good for us.

TUMINAH: (*To the* CANDIDATES) OK, girls, you're in! Come back in three days and we'll put you up and supply you with whatever you need. Work will start on the 15th of next month.

              (*The three embrace happily, ask permission to leave, and then exit.* TUMINAH *then speaks to* BAJENET.)

              Anyone else to interview?

BAJENET: Just one more. Here's her file. Pretty, isn't she?

TUMINAH: Tell her to come in. (*Wearily*) Fifteen candidates we interviewed today.... I had no idea how tiring and boring this job could be.

BAJENET: Maybe because that's you're a woman. I like this part of the job. Want me to call her in?

TUMINAH: Yes, let's get this over with.

BAJENET: (*Calling out*) It's your turn now. (*Handing a file to* TUMINAH) Her name is Dewi.

              (*A young woman enters. She looks nervous.*)

TUMINAH: (*Reading from the file*) Name: Dewi. Age: 18. Vocational school graduate, once taught kindergarten. Father, a farmer. Mother, a *jamu* seller. Born in Blora. Came to Jakarta to work but was swindled by the agent. Gave him Rp. 300,000 for papers to work in Saudi Arabia but four months later still hadn't received them. Was kept in a home...

DEWI: Kidnapped. Locked up was more like it.

TUMINAH: Whatever.... Escaped and was rescued by the police. Went to live in Ciputat with her aunt and uncle and their nine children. Is this all correct?

DEWI: Yes, Ma'am.

TUMINAH: Don't call me "Ma'am." My name is Tuminah. You can call
             me that.

DEWI: Yes, Ma'am.

TUMINAH: Why do you want to work as a prostitute? You know the
             risks, don't you?

DEWI: I don't know what else to do. After being locked up like
             that, I don't know what to do. (*Crying, barely able to talk*)
             I'm too ashamed to go back home. My folks think I'm
             working abroad.

TUMINAH: So?

DEWI: So I don't want to make my aunt's life any harder. It's hard
             enough as is. And one night her husband, my uncle....
             (*Crying.*)

BAJENET: Tried to rape you? Is that it?

DEWI: (*Crying all the more*) Yes. So now I don't have anything and
             don't know where to go.

BAJENET: (*Whispering to* TUMINAH) Same old story. I hear it all the
             time. But whether it's the truth doesn't much matter. What's
             important is that she's pretty.

             (*Suddenly a commotion is heard and then another young
             woman,* ANTJE, *who is decked out to the max, stomps in
             angrily. The guard, whose name is* BONAR, *is unable to stop
             her.*)

ANTJE: I just heard from Adé that you were interviewing today.
             Son-of-a-bitch. I put in my application, all proper and like.
             How come nobody called me?

BONAR: Sorry, Boss, I couldn't stop her.

ANTJE: I really want this job. I swear. Did the other girls bribe you? Is that why I wasn't called. I have the experience: seven years of it! And I'm really good at it. Shit! What kind of discrimination is this? You want to test me first, I'm ready. I need this job. I need the money. I can do anything. You want me to work out of town, I will. What do you know of me anyway? Who is doing the testing? Tell me so that I know.

TUMINAH: I am.

ANTJE: Ohhh, but you're a woman.

BONAR: What do you want me to do with this slut? Run her off?

TUMINAH: Let her be, Bonar. You can wait outside.

BONAR: Ok. (*Exits.*)

ANTJE: If you want to test me, Ma'am, I'm up for it. (*Pointing at* BAJENET) I can do it with that guy if you want to see what I can do.

TUMINAH: What's your name?

ANTJE: I'm Antje, from Kebon Kawung. This work is easy for me. I can do it while fanning myself. I'm only twenty-four. Tell me what to do and I'll do it.

TUMINAH: What do you think, Bajenet?

ANTJE: No need to think about it! Take me and you won't regret it.

BAJENET: Alright, you're hired. Now go home and we'll get back to you.

ANTJE: You're not messing with me, are you? Watch if you are. I'll chase you down to the end of the world and burn that moustache of yours.

BAJENET: Enough already. Go home. We'll contact you.

ANTJE: OK, I'll go now. (BAJENET *puts his hand on her behind.*) Oh my, copping a little feel, are you? Well, that's alright as long as I'm in. By the way, was Adé accepted?

BAJENET: Yes, she was. (*Calling*) Bonar!

BONAR: (*Entering*) Yes, boss?

BAJENET: Escort the two women to the street and give them some transport money.

BONAR: Yes, boss. Come on.

DEWI: Help me, Tuminah, I need the job.

BONAR: You're in but now you got to go.

(BONAR, DEWI *and* ANTJE *exit.*)

BAJENET: Boy, that last one, Antje, was high on something for sure. Now you see, Tuminah, this is the kind of work I have to do every day: dealing with weirdoes. After a while though, you get used to it. So how many was that we accepted. Seven?

TUMINAH: What about Antje?

BAJENET: Forget that one. Tomorrow we'll have moved anyway. She can bitch all she likes when she comes here and finds this is someone else's office. But Dewi is in, right? (TUMINAH *nods*) OK, I'll get going now. (*Exits with personnel folders.*)

TUMINAH: Dear God, seeing those girls is like looking at myself in the mirror. That's what I once went through. Alone and hopeless with nothing to hold on to, but I had to live. No one cared. And when someone did want to help, it wasn't from their heart but from what they could get from me in return. (*Crying, then singing an old song from "Time Bomb."*)

For a worm like me, is there another choice
when all that is offered is poison?
Is there another choice?

Here and there is only poison;
Is there another choice?
Oh, is there another choice?

(DUING *enters hastily with* BAJENET *on his tail.*)

DUING: Bad news, Tuminah, bad news, bad news, bad news.

TUMINAH: What is it?

DUING: It's bad, it's bad.

TUMINAH: Well, what is it? Tell me straight!

DUING: The trans were taken to the police station. All of them!

TUMINAH: Nothing strange about that. The police are always staging raids and hauling them in.

DUING: But it wasn't a raid.

TUMINAH: Well, what was it then?

DUING: They're being put through that 4-H course. That's dangerous, isn't it?

BAJENET: So what if they go through that course. What's it to us?

DUING: But Ike and Laila were among them. If they were to say anything about us, that could be dangerous. Laila is one of Tibal's regulars, after all.

TUMINAH: (*Interjecting*) You're right. If they were to open their mouths, it would be bad for us.

BAJENET: We need to report this to Tibal and Roima.

TUMINAH: Yeah, that Laila she has very loose lips.

(*All exit.*)

LIGHTS CHANGE

10

Night at the home of the government OFFICIAL. *The official's* WIFE *is speaking to* POLICE 1 *and* POLICE 2.

WIFE: Do you know what time it is? It's 10 PM and my husband is not well! If you have something to report, can't it wait until morning?

POLICE 1: But this is important, Ma'am, and the boss told us to report any important information as soon as we [?] receive it.

WIFE: But my husband isn't well and can't be bothered.

POLICE 1: Please, Ma'am, we really need to see him.

WIFE: Are you the boss in this town or is it my husband? What kind of funny business is this anyway? And what is your rank, by the way?

POLICE 2: Funny business or not, if it's for the job, we'll do it. This is important, Ma'am

(*Before the* WIFE *can answer, the* OFFICIAL, *whose eyes are covered with a black cloth, comes into the room with the* P.A. *and* DOCTOR.)

OFFICIAL: What is all this commotion about?

POLICE 1: We have something to report, sir.

OFFICIAL: What is it? I don't have time for this.

POLICE 1: It's all in this report sir. (*Handing a large spiral bound report to the* OFFICIAL) Three hundred pages which I typed myself.

WIFE: Are you joking! You're asking my husband to read a 300 page report? Can't you see he has an eye problem. Do you want him to go blind?

POLICE 2:   If that's what's necessary for the job, Ma'am. But if he can't read 300 pages, he can go straight to the conclusion on the final page.

OFFICIAL: Paijo, read the important part on the last page.

PAIJO: Yes, sir. (*Taking the report and opening it to the last page*) Conclusion: The gang once led by Kumis has risen again and is now under the leadership of Tibal and Roima.

OFFICIAL: Stop. Those two names ring a bell.

PAIJO: They are the two who led the demonstration the trannies staged outside your office ten years ago. It was after that demonstration you erected a statue in honor of the tranny who was killed by a stray bullet.

OFFICIAL: That's right. Those two accused me of burning down the prostitution complex. But then they disappeared, as if they'd been swallowed by the earth.

WIFE: (*Jealous*) And Tuminah, too! You only pretend to have forgotten her. As if I didn't know.

OFFICIAL: Dear, would you stop bringing that up. I've changed. How many times must I ask for your forgiveness?

WIFE: It's only because you got caught with your pants down you asked forgiveness. If you hadn't, you'd have gone on for sure.

OFFICIAL: This is a business matter, dear; let's not mix it up with domestic affairs.

WIFE: (*To the* POLICEMEN) Wipe out that gang. It doesn't matter the cost. These are my husband's orders. And drag in that woman by the name of Tuminah. I want to look that shameless female rhino in the eye. Now go.

POLICE 1:   And your orders, sir?

OFFICIAL: You just heard them. Exactly what my wife said.

POLICE 2:   But sir, don't you want to read the report first? It's really interesting, almost like a romance.

OFFICIAL: What the hell!? Does your rank permit you to give orders to me? I have your report and I will read it but my order for you now is to wipe out that gang. What more are you waiting for?

POLICE 1:   (*Afraid*) Yes, sir. Yes, sir.

OFFICIAL: That gang, whomever they are, is causing public unrest. We are government employees, paid by the people, whose job it is to make people feel safe. Do you understand? Use whatever means you need to eradicate that gang. Paijo will issue an official order in the morning. Understood?

POLICE 1:   Understood, sir.

OFFICIAL: Now get out of here and don't show your faces before you succeed. If you fail, I'll report this to your superior and the two of you could be accused of aiding or: and have the two of you accused of aiding and abetting them. Understood?

POLICE 1:   Understood, sir.

OFFICIAL: Now leave.

POLICE 1:   Yes, sir!

              (*They exit quickly.*)

OFFICIAL: Damn, damn, damn! My eyes, Doctor, they hurt even more than before...

DOCTOR: You have to calm now. Getting angry just makes them hurt all the more.

WIFE: That and thinking about Tuminah.

OFFICIAL: Please, dear! I'd completely forgotten her and then you bring it up again. I swear that for me there is no other woman greater than you.

WIFE: Bullshit. That's what you say now but when you see a pair of smooth cheeks, you say something else. One good thing about those sick eyes of yours is that you can't ogle anymore. (*Exits.*)

OFFICIAL: Dear, dear...

P.A.:   She's gone, sir.

OFFICIAL: Ridiculous. (*To the* DOCTOR) How many days have I been like this?

DOCTOR: Ten, sir.

OFFICIAL: It feels like a year.

LIGHTS CHANGE

11

Nethertime [?] at the third gateway to the third building. Circles of light, like laser bursts, flash in the sky. Party music can be heard. The GUIDE *and* JULINI *arrive at the third gateway where two heavenly* GUARDS *are busy at their personal computers. One is checking numbers and flow charts; the other is playing super Nintendo.*

GUIDE: We're here now, at the gateway to the building called "One Sun and A Million Lightning Bolts." My job ends here. Once you go through the gateway, another guide will take you to your destination. Any questions before I go?

JULINI: Is Roima there?

GUIDE & JULINI: (*In unison*) I can't say.

JULINI: After going through the gateway, what am I to do?

GUIDE & JULINI: (*In unison*) I can't say.

JULINI: What's the point of this journey?

GUIDE & JULINI: (*In unison*) I can't say.

JULINI: Why do I even bother asking questions when that's the only answer I get?! Get out of here!

GUIDE: Good bye, Julini.

JULINI: No need for goodbyes. A waste of time.

GUIDE: Good bye, Julini. Your journey is still a long one and will take you through a sea of soy sauce, a plain of fire, a river of blood, a lake of winds, a mountains of skulls, a bridge of knives, a ladder of cotton, a bottomless well...

JULINI: First you can't talk and now you give a speech. Jeez, just scram, would ya?

GUIDE: I feel sorry for you, Julini, because your journey will never end.

JULINI: God, you drive me up the wall. Are you going to leave or not?

GUIDE: I feel sorry for you, Julini. Your destiny is written.

(*The* GUIDE *exits. Left alone,* JULINI *now looks around and notices the two* GUARDS *seated on high.*)

JULINI: (*Calling*) Hey, hey, you up there! Hey, guards! (*No response*) Must be deaf or something. Well then, I'll just go in.

(JULINI *steps into the gateway but suddenly a million light rays stop her and she is thrown back outside and to the ground.*)

What the fuck.... What's going on? I was told to go in and now I can't. (*To the* GUARDS) Hey, hey you! Guards! (*No response*) This is as crazy as the instructions to get here. How come I can't go inside?

(JULINI *tries to enter again but a million light rays throw her back outside and to the ground.*)

Ow, ow, what the hell...

(*Finally, the* GUARDS *take notice of her.*)

GUARD 1:   Hello! Who are you?

JULINI: My name is Julini.

GUARD 1:   What are you doing here?

JULINI: Ain't that the question! When I woke up, I was dressed in this wedding outfit and then I was brought here. I don't know why I was brought here. I was only told that I was to meet my groom. So, where is he? Where is he?

GUARD 1:   (*To the other* GUARD) Check the roll. See if the name "Julini" is there.

GUARD 2:   (*Typing at the keyboard, then looking at the screen of his computer*) Nope. No Julini. But there is a Julino, a delivery from the Guide Number 436290456.

GUARD 1:   (*To* JULINI) Is your name Julino?

JULINI: No, it's Julini.

GUARD 1:   Well, whoever you are, go through the gateway. There you will find instructions on how to get to your destination.

JULINI: And where is that?

GUARD 1:   I can't say.

JULINI: Hmm, just the same.

GUARD 2:   Please step through the gateway.

(JULINI *enters the gateway but yet again is struck by a million rays of light, causing her to stumble backwards.*)

JULINI: What the heck? I'm told to come in but then get tortured.

GUARD 1:   You went through the wrong gateway. Can't you see! There are two: one for women and one for men. You went into the women's gateway and so you were expelled because you're a man.

JULINI: Who says I'm a man? I'm a woman. The whole world knows that I'm a woman.

GUARD 2:   According to the records in this computer, you are a man. Let me read it for you. Name: Bambang Julino. Age: 34. Gender: Male. Marital status: unmarried. Nationality: Hmm, not listed. Religion: Not listed either. Address: Not listed. Cause of death: Killed by a stray bullet. Is that clear now?

JULINI: Yes, it's clear.

GUARD 1:   Then come in through the men's gate.

JULINI: I don't want to. I'm a woman. Ever since I was born, I've felt myself to be a girl and the older I got, the more womanly I felt. All my life, I've only worn dresses. You can't tell me to change just like that. Where is there a guy with such a round ass as mine? Where is there a guy with lips as sexy as mine? Just try to find one. You won't succeed.

(*Suddenly, three figures appear and approach the gateway where* JULINI *is standing. It's* TARSIH, KASIJAH *and* KUMIS.)

GUARD 1:   (*To the three*) Hey, you. You have to register. Who are you?

KUMIS: I'm Kumis.

GUARD 2:   (*Checking the computer*) Yeah, he's here.

TARSIH: I'm Tarsih.

GUARD 2:   Her too.

KASIJAH: My name is Kasijah.

GUARD 2:   Yup, they're all there.

JULINI: (*Calling to the three*) Hey, where have you guys been? How come I got here first?

GUARD 2:   They came without a guide. No wonder they're late. Probably went somewhere else first.

GUARD 1:   (*To the three*) You can go in now.

JULINI: Tarsih, Kasijah, Kumis.... It's me, Julini. You remember me, don't you? You're dead too, aren't you? Hey! Tarsih, Kasijah, Kumis.... It's me, Julini. Come on, say something!

     (*The three completely ignore* JULINI *and with, stiffened movements, go through the gateway.* KUMIS *goes through the men's gate and* TARSIH *and* KASIJAH *go through the women's gate.* JULINI *tries again to get their attention and tails* KASIJAH *and* TARSIH *but while they are able to pass through the gateway* JULINI *is once again thrown back out.*)

JULINI: Ow, that hurt! Come on, I want to go in. They got in, why can't I?

GUARD 2:   Our rules are strict.

JULINI: They're dead too, aren't they?

GUARD 2:   Yes. Tibal murdered Kumis. Kasijah and Tarsih were killed in a fire.

JULINI: So how come they can enter but not I? Why are there two gateways anyway? There should be just one for everyone to pass through, both men and women.

They say, in God's eyes, everyone is the same, both men and women. What distinguishes people are their sins, not gender. That's right, ain't it? Men and women are the same, so what's with these differences then?

GUARD 1:   Are you doubting the rules? These rules have existed since time immemorial and no one has ever protested. As to why there is such a rule, it is not within our authority to answer. It's up to you. You can follow the rules or not.

JULINI: Listen, it's not that I don't want to follow the rules. I've always followed the rules. I'm a woman, you see. I swear. If you don't believe, then test me. Come on, I'll prove to you that I'm a woman.

(JULINI *attempts to climb the gateway to reach the* GUARDS *but is stopped by a millions rays of light and is thrown back to the ground.*)

Ow, ow! Damn it and damn it again. What's with the torture? I just want to go in.

GUARD 1:   It is impossible for you to touch us and you cannot enter if you don't follow the rules. Everything has been laid out from above. To attempt to reject the rules is useless.

(*Party music can be heard coming from inside the gateway.*)

There's a party here today. If you come in, there might still be a place for you.

JULINI: I want to come in but only if you recognize first that I'm a woman.

GUARD 1:   That's not our job. Our job is only to guard the gateway—which is going to close soon for an indefinite period of time.

(*The sound of clapping and singing can be heard. People are singing "The Party Song."*)

VOICES:

Darkness and gloom abound
While everywhere, silence surrounds
Everywhere, there's only hope
But here, light is in abundance
And music, and rice, and weed
You may take as much as you like

Everywhere are dryness and drought
Everything is withered and fallen
Everywhere is thirst
But here, rain is in abundance
Water and wine are free flow
Drink until you are drunk

Everywhere are curses and threats
Everywhere are cries and complaints
Everywhere is only woe and misery
But here there is praise and honor
Laughter, gifts, and flowers
Which make the place even more exciting

Come in and take what you will
Pleasure is waiting here for you
Come in and take what you will
Come in and take what you will

GUARD 1:

Hear that? The party has begun. Come in and have a good time. Don't stand there outside. You won't find anything there.

JULINI:

No. I am Roima's wife. On earth I had nothing except the pride of having Roima for my husband. Even now, I still feel that I am his wife. I'm wearing this wedding dress for him. If I go through the men's gate, I would have to dispose of my pride—which is something I cannot do. You must understand. You make it as hard as getting a proper ID.

(*The singing from inside the gateway grows louder, a cacophony of sound.* JULINI *begins to sing, competing with their song.*)

Who knows anything about me
Except for me myself
All that's said about me
Are only curses and threats
I've had my time in hell on earth
Now I will choose where to go

Who is able to see their true reflection
Except the one looking in the mirror
What do they know what's in my heart
Who knows my feelings and dreams
On earth, I never had a place
Is that the way it is here too?

This door is the right one for me
The other door, I'll not pass
Let me choose the right one for me
With no flattery or deceit
With no pressure or force

GUARD 1:   Well, it's up to you. Just know that here there is no other choice. All is in the plan. Are you coming in or not?

JULINI: No, I refuse. I will not enter until I am recognized as a woman. I'm really a woman, I swear.

GUARD 1:   But not original.

JULINI: Don't look at the outside. Look at the inside, here. Maybe I'm not original, but I'm real. Really! Does that have you confused? What I mean, is that I've long forgotten the falsity and felt my real being. If I go through the men's door, then what about Roima? He's a man.

GUARD 1:   As I said, it's up to you. We're going to close the gate.

JULINI: Then I will stay here. Maybe I'll open up a food stall. Or go back to giving massages like I once did. I will stay here and wait. (*Singing slowly*)

If necessary, I'll wait a thousand years
As long as it's for Roima
Tortured for a thousand years, no matter
As long as it's for Roima

(*The party music stops. It is now still and quiet.*)

LIGHTS CHANGE

12

Evening. On the street. SAWIL *and* BILUN, *who are still dressed in astronaut suits, are still calculating.*

SAWIL: What country do you think we should buy?

BILUN: Ibanga.

SAWIL: What?

BILUN: Ibanga.

SAWIL: What country is that? Where is it? What's its size and population? What's the name of its capital and head of state? I don't think I've ever seen it on a map.

BILUN: Ibanga is a big country in Asia, a maritime nation with massive forests and wild animals—a place of incredible natural wealth that has yet to be exploited. An area almost twice the size of the U.S. mainland with more than 200 million people. Its capital is Katangali. As to its head of state, we're waiting to see the outcome of its ongoing elections. The point is the country has potential but stress the word "potential" because the economy is in collapse as a result of massive corruption. Its educational system is a mess but the people do like soccer and to gamble. They even have a minister especially in charge of gambling.

SAWIL: Wow, that's modern for you. So is it up for sale?

BILUN: I saw an ad for it in *Time* last month.

SAWIL: Any bidders?

BILUN: Lots. All the superpowers would like it.

SAWIL: How much are they asking?

BILUN: (*Taking out the magazine and pointing to a figure*) Here's the minimum bid.

SAWIL: (*Reading*) Is that all? We have the money for that. We should put in a bid fast. Let's calculate this. Let's say we are able to buy it for 10% more than the minimum bid, we could sell it for 20% more than that. How much profit would that give us?

BILUN: (*On the calculator*) 10% of so and so.... And we sell it at 20% higher, here's what we'll make.

SAWIL: Wow, we'll be rich! Let's do this quickly before other people get in there.

BILUN: Do we need cash. I could call the president of the World Bank if we do. I have his Starko number.

SAWIL: No need. Cash would weigh too much. We can use a credit card.

(*They exit quickly.*)

LIGHTS CHANGE

13

Night. At the gang's headquarters. The GANG MEMBERS *have gathered:* ROIMA, TIBAL, TUMINAH, DUING, *and* BAJENET. LAILA *is under interrogation and crying in fear. Several* GANG MEMBERS *are demonstrating their martial arts skills.*

TIBAL: Now you cry. Now you're sorry. What's the use after it's happened? Because of your loose lips, we're all under threat now. You took an oath, remember? Do you remember the most important part? Answer me!

LAILA: To be loyal to the group.

TIBAL: And...? And even more important than that?

LAILA: If you're caught by the police, it's your problem. Don't bring other people into it.

TIBAL: And what did you do? You betrayed us.

LAILA: I didn't mean too, boss, I swear.

TIBAL: What's the sentence for a traitor?

GANG MEMBERS: Death!

LAILA: I'm sorry. Forgive me. (*Crying*) I didn't realize until after I'd spoken. The police were just too smart for me.

TIBAL: Why's that?

LAILA: Well they asked about my customers first and then they asked who was the best and the manliest and I said his name was Tibal.

TIBAL: Fucking son-of-a-bitch. Saying that is enough reason for me to kill you! You're the only one who talked. Wanda didn't say anything. You're a danger if we let you live.

ROIMA: Then what happened, Laila?

LAILA: Then they asked if it was the same Tibal who'd been jailed for killing a security officer. "Why would you ever do it with him?" they asked. So I said, "Why not? He's hot!"

TIBAL: And then you told them everything?

LAILA: (*Crying*) It just came out of my mouth. I know I have loose lips. (*Slapping her own mouth*) Loose lips, loose lips. But I didn't mean to, I swear I didn't!

TIBAL: What's the sentence that she deserves?

LAILA: (*Crying in fright*) Take pity on me! I was able to escape from them. I did that for you. To let you know.

TIBAL: Take pity on you? You're asking for pity when twice now you've almost destroyed us all? Who was it that revealed the location of our meeting place a few months ago? Uh? Who?

LAILA: I know it was me but it wasn't on purpose.

TIBAL: You just happened to tell the policeman you were fucking, right?

LAILA: Yes...

TIBAL: And that wasn't on purpose? That's now easy for you to say. Rules have to be followed. Discipline is the key to success and betrayal is not allowed. You betrayed us and you still want pity? Well, Ok, I'll show you pity. Bajenet!

BLEKI: Yes, boss?

TIBAL: You got that knife of yours.

BAJENET: I got it, boss.

TIBAL: See that box there. (*Pointing to a large box on stage*) Put her inside it.

LAILA: What are you going to do to me? Help me, Roima, help!

	(BAJENET *forces* LAILA *into the box until only her head is visible.*)
TIBAL:	You said you wanted pity so that's what I'm giving you. We're not going to kill you straightway.
	Take off her clothes, Bajenet, and then cut off her dick, bit by bit.
BAJENET:	Yes, boss.
LAILA:	(*Screaming in fright*) Oh my god! Not that! Then what will happen to me? Help me, Roima. Help me. I swear I didn't mean to do it. I know I have a big mouth but I'm not a traitor. Help me.
BAJENET:	(*Laughing*) I haven't done anything and you're already screaming. But this is how it will work: one slice now; a minute later, another slice, and so on until you are dead.
	Funny, isn't it? All this time you've dreamed of not having a dick and wanting to be a woman. Well now I'm going to help you get your wish. How much would an operation like that cost?
LAILA:	I don't want that thing—but, please, not this way. Help me. In an operation, they give you something to put you to sleep.
BAJENET:	I can give you something. A punch! And you're out, just like that.
ROIMA:	(*Unable to restrain himself anymore*) Stop! Stop this, Bajenet, and get out of here.
TIBAL:	Go on and do it, Bajenet!
ROIMA:	Get out, I said. Get out.
	(BAJENET *is confused.*)
TIBAL:	Do what I told you to do, idiot!

ROIMA: I'll kill the first person who touches Laila.

TIBAL: A traitor must be punished. Why are you stopping us?

ROIMA: I agree a traitor must be punished, but what you are doing is not humane. If you want to kill someone, do it quickly. Don't torture someone like that. We're not uncivilized people, you know.

TIBAL: (*Laughing*) Humane? We're criminals and you are worried about being humane?

ROIMA: We may be criminals but we're not insane. If Laila's a traitor and you want to kill her, then kill her, but do it quickly. Where's your dagger, Bajenet? Here. (*Enters the box*) Forgive me, Laila. (*Stabbing* LAILA, *her blood gushes*) Forgive me.

LAILA: Thank you, Roima. (*Dying*) Thank you.

TIBAL: (*At the same time as the above action*) Stop! Wait! Don't kill her yet. (*As* LAILA *expires*) Fuck! You're not a criminal, Roima. You're a fairy.

            (TIBAL *begins to exit angrily.*)

ROIMA: (*Shouting*) Take back what you said, Tibal!

            (TIBAL *stops in his tracks.*)

TIBAL: Or what?

TUMINAH: Tibal, Roima, it's not good to fight in front of the other men.

ROIMA: (*Wearily*) We're never going to see eye to eye.

TIBAL: You got that right, buddy.

            (TIBAL *exits angrily followed by* BAJENET *and* BLEKI.)

ROIMA: (*To the other* GANG MEMBERS) What are you waiting for? Get out of here. Take Laila's body and give her a good burial.

BONAR: When's the next meeting, boss?

ROIMA: We'll let you know. For the time being, stop everything
             you're doing. And tell that to your men.

BONAR: Yes, boss.

             (*The* GANG MEMBERS *exit, dragging with them the box
             that* LAILA *is in.*)

TUMINAH: You too, Duing.

             (DUING *exits quickly.*)

ROIMA: I'm always uncertain, hesitant. I'm not cut out to be a
             leader. I don't have it in me.

TUMINAH: You just need to rest, Roima. You've been working too hard.

ROIMA: There's never rest for people like us. We always have to be
             on guard. Close your eyes one second, and you're gone.

             How can Tibal be so cruel? There's no end to his vengeance.
             Kumis is dead. Tibal killed him and now we're supposed to
             be building a new life for ourselves: for you and me and the
             rest of the gang. We have to be strong. We need each other.

TUMINAH: You're right.

ROIMA: (*Singing*) *Rising from a long sleep*
             Discarding dreams and desires
             Crawling out from the gutter
             Fighting abuse and humiliation
             Who can hold us down
             If we roaches are as one?

             But unity will never be born from vengeance. It must grow
             naturally, from a mutual sense of awareness. That's where
             real strength is found.

We eat what's good for eating
We beat the things that need to be beaten
We tear down what must be torn down
Then rebuild upon the rubble
With work, work, and more work
On the basis of mutual love

That is my dream.

TUMINAH: That's the dream of all the underdogs like ourselves. But you can't do it alone; you need a friend.

ROIMA: You're right; I need lots of friends. Oh, Tuminah, why have things turned out this way? Sometimes I think it was better the way we used to be, fifteen years ago. We were poor then and life was hard but it wasn't complicated like it is now.

TUMINAH: Life is like work but less enjoyable. It just gets keeps getting harder, crazier, and more complicated.

ROIMA: Yeah...

TUMINAH: Can we forget about all this, if only for a moment?

ROIMA: I don't know. My head aches.

TUMINAH: (*Singing*) *Think about the empty sky*
Refreshing and calm
Imagine the laughter of a child
Refreshing and calm
Think only of you and me
Refreshing and calm

ROIMA & TUMINAH: (*Singing together*) *Think only of love*
Refreshing and calm
Refreshing and calm
Imagine there is only
Refreshing and calm

(*Resting his head in* TUMINAH's *lap,* ROIMA *sleeps like a baby.* TUMINAH *stares at him lovingly.*)

LIGHTS CHANGE

14

Night. Gang headquarters. TIBAL *is angry.* BLEKI *and* BAJENET *fan the flames.*

TIBAL: Who was it that killed Kumis? Who should have become the leader of his gang? Who should have become the supreme boss? Me, that's who! But what happened? Roima took over; he got control and I couldn't do anything.

BAJENET: You can't have two captains on a boat.

BLEKI: Maybe you should kill him.

BAJENET: What? Kill who?

BLEKI: Nothing. That just slipped out.

TIBAL: Bleki, come here. (BLEKI *is frightened*) Don't be scared. Sometimes you can be brilliant. And you, Bajenet, what you said is also true: a boat can't have two captains. But can I trust the two of you?

BAJENET: I've always been faithful to you.

BLEKI: Me too.

TIBAL: Good. Then let's make a plan to get rid of Roima.

BAJENET: What about Tuminah?

TIBAL: Tuminah is my kid sister. I raised her. Don't worry about her. The thing now is to get rid of Roima. But I'll need your help. Let's talk about this somewhere else.

(TIBAL *exits, followed by* BLEKI *and* BAJENET.)

LIGHTS CHANGE

15

Night. At the government OFFICIAL'*s home. The* OFFICIAL *is still wearing a blindfold. His* WIFE *is berating two* POLICEMEN. *The* P.A. *is also present.*

WIFE: What kind of policemen are you. It's obvious that the tranny who escaped is connected with that gang of criminals. How could you let her escape? You two are going to have to pay for this. (*To the* P.A.) Take down their badge numbers and arrange for their dismissal.

P.A.: Noted.

WIFE: So now where are you going to get the information? Who can tell you where their hideout is located. And where Tuminah is hiding? Answer me.

POLICE 2: Excuse me, Ma'am, but who's the one that should be cussing us out? You or your husband.

OFFICIAL: Shut your mouth. Her voice is the same as mine. She is my voice as long as I am sick. Obey her.

POLICE 2: Yes, sir. Sorry. We'll obey.

WIFE: For the public good, I am willing to take on this job. If I weren't thinking about my husband's job, you could die for all I care.

POLICE 1: I know we were wrong, Ma'am.

WIFE: That's obvious. No need to say it.

POLICE 1: So what are we supposed to do, Ma'am?

WIFE:	Well, if you don't want to get fired, you'll have to work harder. Arrest anyone connected with Tuminah and that gang. All of them! I want to see their faces.
POLICE 2:	But how, Ma'am?
OFFICIAL:	What kind of stupid question is that. You are officers of the law; it's your job to know. You got to do something for your paycheck.
POLICE 1:	I have a plan, sir.
OFFICIAL:	Tell me, what is it.
POLICE 1:	Those criminals are close with the trannies. We'll arrest all the trannies in the city and then interrogate them.
POLICE 2:	They really are the cause of disruption.
WIFE:	(*To her husband, the* OFFICIAL) This is all your fault. What good did it do you giving into their demand to build a mausoleum for what's her name, that tranny who got shot.
POLICE 2:	Julini, Ma'am.
WIFE:	I don't care what her name is. But what you did, dear, only served to whip them up all the more. I say, tear down that mausoleum and the statue too. It's pornographic is what it is. It's a blight on the cityscape.
POLICE 2:	I agree, Ma'am. The area has become a nest of evil. Trannies, whores, and criminals gather there. Regular people are afraid to go there. It's scary there.
OFFICIAL:	OK, I agree with your plan to arrest all the trannies. But, hey, wait, aren't some of them in a 4-H course now?

POLICE 1:	It just finished but they wouldn't have gone too far.
WIFE:	Do whatever you need to do put those criminals out of action.
OFFICIAL:	I give you two weeks. If you fail, you'll be fired. If you succeed, you'll go up in rank.
POLICE 1:	Yes, sir.
OFFICIAL:	Now leave.
POLICE 2:	And that statue of the super-tranny hero? Do you want us to tear it down, sir?
OFFICIAL:	That's not your business. Now leave.
POLICE 2:	Yes, sir. (*Exits with* POLICE 1.)
WIFE:	An easy a job that and they're still fools. (*Exits.*)
OFFICIAL:	How long have my eyes been this way, Paijo?
P.A.:	Going into the fourth month, sir. Exactly ninety-nine days.
OFFICIAL:	(*Moaning*) I don't feel I can do this anymore. Life should be more peaceful but it keeps getting worse all the time. I want to tender my resignation.
P.A.:	Oh, no, don't sir. What would happen to me?
OFFICIAL:	The chief requirement for a government official is that he be in good mental and physical health. But look at me, I'm blind. I don't meet that requirement anymore. Worse still, I'd be ashamed if my condition were to come to light.

LIGHTS CHANGE

16

Night. Beneath the statue of Julini. The TRANSWOMEN *are singing "The Shemale Song.")*

TRANSWOMEN: *Don't think that we are blind*
That we don't know what's behind the wall
We know how much you own
We know just what you plan

Don't think we will stay silent
Pale and pallid from fright
We know what you are eating
We even know the color of your shit

Your speeches are sweet and fiery
Speaking of equal justice for all
Your advice is firm and inspiring
Speaking of eradication of poverty

But can you see what is happening
Behind the wall
We know
Even the color of your shit

But don't you worry
And do not be so suspicious
Now we stand as one
In support of you
Because we are afraid

(TÉA comes running in, arms flailing her arms, looking distraught, causing the TRANSWOMEN *to immediately stop singing.)*

TÉA: Help, help, oh my god, oh my go...

IKE: What is it, Téa? You're like a mouse running from a cat.

ESYI: Or someone smeared chilies on your tush!

SYENI: Did a customer stiff you?

TÉA: (*Crying*) It's Laila, Laila...

IKE: Did you have another fight with Laila?

TÉA: I just saw her, I saw her, oh, my god...

IKE: Come on, finish the story before you start crying. What is it?

TÉA: But I'm so sad, so sad. I've been crying since earlier, ever since I saw Laila's corpse...

            (*All the* TRANSWOMEN *scream.*)

IKE: Her corpse? Laila's dead?

ESYI: But she just went through that 4-H course. How could she be dead?

TÉA: I came across Bajenet and Bleki picking up her rotting corpse. They said Roima killed her.

IKE: That's not possible. I can't believe Roima would do that.

TÉA: I swear it's true. Poor Laila, she hadn't paid off her bra yet. And now I don't have anyone to fight with...

IKE: Where did they find her corpse?

TÉA: At the Kuningan water gate.

IKE: Let's go there and see.

            (*All exit.*)

LIGHTS CHANGE

17

Night. A Jakarta street. SAWIL *and* BILUN *appear. Both are very angry.*

SAWIL: There has to be something wrong here; somebody is playing games. We couldn't have lost the tender. How much of a percentage did the U.S. bribe the tender committee?

BILUN: Thirty percent. But we offered fifteen. I told you we should have brought cash but you didn't want to. If they had seen ten trucks full of cash, that would have caught their eye.

SAWIL: This is an insult to traders. That's what we are, aren't we? The U.S. wants to buy the country for itself and probably use it as a site to test their nuclear bombs. The poor people of Ibanga. Where will their 200 million people go? The North Pole?

Damn it to hell. What other country is on the market? We have to get in there fast—and bring cash, if necessary. How much do we need to print?

BILUN: Here, look at this advertisement. For rent: The country of Blenggutu. Includes full air-conditioning, a three-car garage, a swimming pool, two servants' rooms.... What the...! Oh, sorry, I was reading the wrong ad.

SAWIL: Here, let me read it. For rent: The country of Blenggutu, population 15 million people, with an area as big as Australia whose capital is...

(POLICEMEN 1 & 2 *enter*)

Hey, it's you two again.

POLICE 2:   Get out of here. Now what are you trying to sell?

SAWIL: We're not trying to sell. We're trying to buy a country. Here, read this ad.

POLICE 2:   Get out of here. I could shoot the both of you. If you're going to be crazy why can't you be normal crazy. You want to buy a country? As if a snail could buy a country. You two don't have enough money to buy land for your graves.

SAWIL: (*To* BILUN) Obviously, they don't know our capability. (*To the* POLICEMEN) You guys wait. The next time we see you we will own the ground you're walking on. And then I will grind you into food for dogs. (*Exits.*)

POLICE 2:   What did you say? You're dead!

POLICE 1:   Calm down. If you deal with crazies, you'll go crazy yourself.

POLICE 2:   They insulted an officer of the law. I'm pissed; that's now twice today this has happened. This morning, the official's wife; now, those crazy guys. Whose orders are we supposed to follow anyway? The official or his wife?

POLICE 1:   His wife. That's normal isn't it? The official is sick, after all.

POLICE 2:   But he must have a number two.

POLICE 1:   Even so, wouldn't his wife know more about her husband's work?

POLICE 2:   But I won't take it. How can she get mad at us? If she were the boss and ordered me to clean the latrines, I'd do it. She should be dealing with women's affairs, not bawling us out.

POLICE 1:   Do what she says. Better that than getting fired. Hey, it's awfully quite here. Where have all the trannies gone. And why did you bring a machine gun? Are you planning on going to war or something? What are you? Rambo? A pistol would have been enough. You better watch what you're doing with that gun.

POLICE 2:   But look at what criminals are using today. Some are even using bombs. This is just to be on the safe side.

POLICE 1:   But you like to get drunk, and when you do, you don't know how to handle yourself. You're drunk already.

POLICE 2:   I'm not drunk. I've only had seven bottles of beer. That's normal.

POLICE 1:   Being drunk on the job is an offense, you know?

POLICE 2:   I know but don't act so high and mighty. How about if we go that palm-wine stall and get something to drink now. I know you're frustrated too, being cussed at by that woman.

POLICE 1:   Shut your mouth and stand up straight. Watch what you're doing with that thing. But, hey, maybe that's not such a bad idea. The waitress there is super sexy.

POLICE 2:   I'm ready to carry out your orders.

              (*The two laughing and then sing "Fucked Up."*)

              What's the use of feeling down
              You just age all the more quickly
              What's the use of taking things to heart
              That only makes you die faster
              Police are like eggs on a wall
              That will break if they fall
              What's the fun in being silent
              When failure or success, it's all the same

              (*They stagger as they exit.* ROIMA *then enters and stands beneath the statue of* JULINI.)

ROIMA: I'm here, Jul. I'm sure you know why I've come. I can't ever forget you. Because of me, you're gone. Because of me, you were shot. I'm so sorry. I was stupid never to have thanked you. All that I have now is because of you. Before I could return your help, you were already dead.

(The statue of JULINI *comes to life and goes to* ROIMA.*)*

JULINI: Roima, honey... Roima...

ROIMA: Jul, is that you? Am I seeing things?

JULINI: No, no, you're not seeing things. I'm here with you. I came because I know that you miss me.

ROIMA: Is this a dream?

JULINI: It's not a dream. Kiss me if you don't believe it. (ROIMA *kisses* JULINI) You see! Still that smell of stink beans.

ROIMA: It really is you. I can touch you, hold you. But you died, didn't you?

JULINI: Who said I was dead? I was just hiding is all. I wanted to test your love, to see if it's as deep as the sea or as shallow as a gutter. In fact, you do still remember me, even though you now have Tuminah at your side. Ten years feels like a century but you are still the man I once knew: ever so masculine, a real Marlboro man.

ROIMA: I still can't believe this is true.

JULINI: It is true but it's also a dream. It's a dream but also true. The point is, reversible like glass, seen from whichever side it's still visible. Hey, do you still like to do it before breakfast?

ROIMA: Don't talk dirty, Jul. This is a serious conversation.

JULINI: I am serious; I've always been serious. Do you still love me?

ROIMA: I still think of you. If that's love, I don't know but, for me, there's no one who compares to you—even if you have the looks of a night owl.

JULINI: Oh, that's what I like. You always talk straight. And maybe I'm not the prettiest thing but I do give you satisfaction, don't I?

ROIMA: Can you forgive me, Jul? I always feel guilty, that it was my fault.

JULINI: What happened wasn't your fault. There's nothing for me to forgive. In my eyes, you're innocent.

ROIMA: (*Crying*) But what happened was my fault! If you hadn't died, we'd still be happy for sure. We would have gotten the money you needed for a sex change operation and then we could have gotten married. Two times we tried but couldn't. Don't leave me now. I don't want to fail again.

JULINI: Your words make me happy, Roima. Happy and moved at the same time. This is what I have waited for. It is impossible to separate the two of us. We are Romeo and Juliet, Layla and Majnun, Roromendut and Pronocitro. We are Romi and Juli, so happy together.

(BLEKI *and* BAJENET *sneak in towards* ROIMA. JULINI *vanishes.*)

BLEKI: (*Covering* ROIMA *with a gunny sack*) I got him!

ROIMA: Who are you? What do you want?

BLEKI: Now, boss! Fast, before he can get away.

(TIBAL *quickly moved towards* ROIMA *with a dagger in his hand.*)

TIBAL: This is where I killed Kumis and this is where I am going to kill you, Roima! (*Stabbing* ROIMA *multiple times*) With you gone, there will be no one to stop me now. I will be the leader, the most powerful gangster, the godfather of 'em all. (*Removing the sack from* ROIMA's *head*) Look at my face, Roima. Take a good look! This is our world—full of treachery and blood—something you can't change. Our kind of people are rough-and-ready, uneducated, from the sticks. We live our lives at the end of the dagger. Whoever is strong will be in power.

ROIMA: (*Breathing heavily*) You're wrong, Tibal. Soon you'll see the gang fall apart. You're angry with only vengeance in your mind. You're not made to be a leader. You're greedy and greed is going to be the end of you. (*Singing slowly*)

Who can hold us back
When the cockroaches unite.

BAJENET: He's a goner, boss.

BLEKI: Yeah, boss, finish him off.

TIBAL: (*Stabbing* ROIMA *one more time*) Goodbye, Roima, and good riddance.

(ROIMA *dies.*)

BAJENET: Now what?

TIBAL: Now we spread the news that Roima was killed by the cops. Drag him to the river and throw him but weigh him down with stones so that he doesn't float away. Then, when we fish him out, it will be like we just happened to find him. Go now.

(*They exit with* ROIMA's *corpse.*)

LIGHTS CHANGE

18

Night. Somewhere. A MADAM, *the brothel manager is giving her* PROSTITUTES *a lesson in etiquette.* TUMINAH *looks on. The atmosphere is raucous and raunchy.*

MADAM: Come on, Dewi, Eva, and Adé, that's not the way to walk. You look like street peddlers with loads on your back. With the kind of rates we charge, you're supposed to be high class. Move your hips as gracefully as possible. When you move your legs, it should look like you're dancing. And your arms shouldn't be stiff like; they should be supple. Tilt your head a bit, look in a particular direction, and smile. Never forget to smile. Smile!

Now try it again. If you follow my instructions, you will look sexy. Clients will go crazy and your rates can go up. Try it again: one, two, three, four...

That's better. Always remember, a good call girl is a good salesgirl. You are salesgirls and what are you selling? Your bodies. Which means, never fall in love. It messes up your careers. Isn't that right, Tuminah?

TUMINAH: That's right.

MADAM: So always remember the Number one rule: never fall in love. Number two: never talk about money. Emphasize service. Satisfactory service produces money like rain. Number three: take care of your bodies. That is very important because your body is your main capital. Once you've learned all the rules of posture and etiquette then I will teach you about art.

(*The* PROSTITUES *break into laughter.*)

Hey, what are you laughing about? If you are high class, art is an important subject of discussion. You need to know how to sing; you have to read poetry; you need to know what novels are bestsellers. After that, it will be lessons on how to speak. Language is important too.

ADÉ: Language? Important? Usually, when a guy is banging on you all he has to say is "Ah, ah, ah" or, at most, give a little scream.

MADAM: Hey, listen to me. When you are pretending to have an orgasm, speak in English. That will impress them.

SRI: (*Pretending to be with a client*) Oh my god, that's right, go on, go on, faster, faster. Wow, that's good. Shit man...

(*They all laugh.*)

MADAM: Yes, like that, but without saying the word "shit," OK? When you go to a client's room, don't immediately take off your clothes. Engage your trick in conversation. Share a drink; make him calm and comfortable. And try to work it so that he doesn't take off his own clothes. That's something for you to do together. You take off his clothes; he takes off yours. Turn on some soft music. Stroke his cheeks and neck.

EVA: But usually they just want to go right to it.

MADAM: That's why you must try to calm him down first. If it's just bang-bang-bang, well that's what they do with their wives. They're coming to you for a different kind of experience, a desire to enter a world of fantasy. Serve him and help his fantasies become true and the next time he comes, he will be coming to find you. Got it?

ALL: Got it!

(DUING *comes running inside.*)

DUING: Tuminah! Tuminah! We have to go. Oh, this is terrible. We have to go now!

TUMINAH: What is it, Duing? What?

DUING: I can't say yet. It's Roima. We have to go now.

TUMINAH: Roima? What's happened to Roima?

DUING:	You have to see for yourself. I can't speak.
	(TUMINAH *exits nervously with* DUING.)
MADAM:	Shall we go on? We'll continue out back. (ALL *follow as the* MADAM *exits*) The client is king, the boss…

LIGHTS CHANGE

19

Night. The TRANSWOMEN *are gathered beneath the Statue of Julini. They are frightened and confused.*

IKE:	First Laila, now Roima. Didn't I say Roima couldn't have been so cruel? The proof is Roima's now a victim too. There must be someone behind this.
TÉA:	But who could have done it?
ESYI:	I heard it was a cop.
WANDA:	Oh my god.
IKE:	A cop?
SYENI:	We have to do something. We have to report this.
IKE:	But report it to whom.
SYENI:	I don't know but we have to report it.
WANDA:	The only cop who could do such a thing is a bad apple. A real cop or government official provides protection and service, not this kind of horrific thing.
	(*The two* POLICEMEN *appear. Both are very drunk.*)
ESYI:	Here they come. Oh my, I wet myself again.
POLICE 2:	Is everyone here? Line up in a neat row and then get into

	the truck over there. Fast.
IKE:	Why should we get into that truck?
POLICE 2:	Don't give me lip. This is a raid.
TÉA:	A raid? But we already took that 4-H course, and now there's a raid?
POLICE 1:	Just do what you're told and get into the truck.
IKE:	Then what are you going to do to us? Kill us one by one? You're just trying to trick us.
POLICE 2:	Nothing is going to happen to you. You're only going to be questioned. If it turns out you have no connection with that criminal gang, we'll let you go.
IKE:	You're lying. You're intending to kill us. I know it.
ESYI:	(*To* IKE) Do you want to make a break for it?
IKE:	Where would we go? Better to resist than to be run down. For Julini, we will protest!
	(*The* TRANSWOMEN *begin to resist the* POLICE.)
POLICE 2:	Hey! Don't you see; I have a gun here!
IKE:	So what? A worm is going to squirm when stepped on, even more so a tranny.
SYENI:	And we've been squirming since before, especially after seeing that moustache of yours.
TÉA:	Attack! For Laila and for Roima.
	(*Their resistance lasts for just a minute.* POLICE 2 *fires his machine gun. The* TRANSWOMEN *hide behind the Julini Statue while screaming. The Julini Statue is shattered and falls. Then the* TRANSWOMEN *fall dead, one by one.*)
POLICE 2:	Ok, who else wants to try!? Who else?! (*Pauses*) Hey, it's quiet here.

POLICE 1:   Maybe they're asleep.

POLICE 2:   What now? Do we wait for them to wake up or drag them to the van?

POLICE 1:   Wait... I think they're dead.

POLICE 2:   How can that be? I shot in the air.

POLICE 1:   But you didn't. Look at that blood. They really are dead. No one is breathing. This one is staring at us.

POLICE 2:   How could that have happened? Really, I swear, I shot in the air.

POLICE 1:   Didn't I tell you not to bring that gun. Now look at what has happened. Who's going to take the blame for this. We've had it now.

POLICE 2:   (*Rubbing his eyes*) Look…. Look at all the butterflies, flying to the sky.

POLICE 1:   Where did they come from? There are so many of them.

              (*The corpses of the* TRANSWOMEN *turn into butterflies and fly to the sky, flapping their wings gracefully. A million butterflies fly to sky while singing "Song of a Million Butterflies."*)

ALL: *Unfurl our wings, slowly move*
              Our bodies so light, we fly
              Rising through the clouds
              Towards the center of the sky

              Where we will not be refused
              Not by the sky

              A million butterflies cover the sky
              Their wings reflect light
              Carrying with them just one hope
              Going to the center of happiness

Where we will not be refused
The sky will not reject us

(*Before disappearing, they attack* POLICE 1 & 2.)

POLICE 1:   Help! Help! They're attacking me. This is all because of you. I told you not to bring a gun. We weren't supposed to kill them.

POLICE 2:   Help! Help! They're eating my gun. They're attacking me!

(*The two* POLICE *run away and then, finally, the butterflies rise into the sky.*)

LIGHTS CHANGE

20

Night. Plaza Julini. At the same moment, screams are heard and flames appear in the distance, followed by the sound of heavy gunshot. TUMINAH *enters, crying and screaming with* DUING *beside her. The Julini Mausoleum is in ruins.*

DUING: Wait, Tuminah, wait! What are you doing, coming here? Look at all those corpses. Whose are they? We have to get out of here. Don't cry here. OMG, the smell is awful.

TUMINAH: (*Screaming*) Roima, why did you have to die? What did you do wrong? Who killed you? We never got the chance to find true happiness, and now you're gone.

(TUMINAH *begins to slowly sing "Tuminah's Song."* TIBAL *enters looking downcast.*)

Think only of the empty sky
Cool and calm
Imagine only a child's laugh
Cool and calm

Think only of you and me
Cool and calm
Think only of love and care
Cool and calm

TIBAL: You have to stop thinking about Roima; he's dead now. And now we have to take revenge on those who have done this to us.

Do you see those flames in the distance? It's a sign that our movement has begun. Our people are on the move, throughout the city. They will all gather here. There will be riots and unrest, commotion and disturbance everywhere.

And when that happens, we will take control, full control, Tuminah—you and I. There will be nobody to humiliate us. There will be none of that anymore. That's been my dream ever since I got out of jail

TUMINAH: I hate this. I hate all of this. (*Exits running.*)

DUING: (*Chasing after*) Tuminah! Tuminah! Don't leave me here.

(BAJENET *enters covered with blood.*)

TIBAL: What are you doing here?

BAJENET: We need to stop the movement, boss. We're overpowered. Roima was right. We moved too soon.

BONAR: (*Entering out of breath*) Boss, boss.... Tibal!

TIBAL: What are you doing here? I told you to watch headquarters.

BONAR: We're done for, boss. There are thirty army trucks surrounding us.

(*Sound of an explosion, then another one.* BLEKI *runs in screaming.*)

BLEKI: Boss, Tibal…. Where are you, boss?

BAJENET: That explosion came from our headquarters. We're done for.

TIBAL: Fuck it! Peabrains, all of you, just like Kumis. We have to be on the move. It's no big deal when people like us die. No one cries for us. We have no choice but to chomp down. If not, we're dead. Come on, follow me, Bajenet, Bonar. We will keep on moving, underground.

(TIBAL *exits followed by* BAJENET.)

LIGHTS CHANGE

21

Night. The home of the OFFICIAL. *The* OFFICIAL *and his* WIFE *are angry with* POLICE 1 *and* 2.

WIFE: What have you ever contributed to the city except unrest? Look at the results. Just look! What were you doing playing around with a machine gun like that? You think you're macho? You want to be Rambo? You look like a clown but act like a big shot. Look at that. There are fires everywhere. And who is responsible? You damn fools.

You do these kinds of things and my husband has to pay for it. He has to take responsibility. What's your answer to that? Don't even bother answering. There's no use anymore. The milk has been tainted by ink. Fools. Brains in your ass.

P.A.:   (*Entering quickly*) They're on the move, sir. They're all on the move.

WIFE: What's on the move? Your ass? Speak clearly.

P.A.:   We don't have to worry. Help is on the way. The military has the gang's headquarters surrounded. According to the military commander, this isn't a big riot. He guarantees that in two or three hours the city will be back under control.

WIFE: That's a relief. Thank heavens the military was on guard and able to act quickly.

P.A.: It appears that unrest broke out in a number of cities simultaneously. But they weren't well organized. Amateurs. It's not even apparent who is in control.

WIFE: The point is, do whatever to make this city safe and stable again. And you two, you'll get what you deserve when the situation is safe again. Now get out of here.

POLICE 1 & 2: (*Simultaneously, as they exit*) Yes, sir.

OFFICIAL: (*Crying with pain*) Ohhh, ohhh, I can't bear it any longer. Help me, help me. I don't have the strength left. I can't see. I can't do anything. All this is my fault. It's my fault...

WIFE: It's probably that Tuminah of yours who's given you the clap or worse.

OFFICIAL: Her again. The same every day. I'm fed up. (*Exits.*)

(*His* WIFE *and* P.A. *chase after him.*)

LIGHTS CHANGE

22

At the third gateway, "One Sun a Million Lightning Bolts." The two heavenly GUARDS *are still squatting there.* JULINI *is on a silence strike.* LAILA *enters.*

LAILA: Heavens my, what am I doing here? What's that gateway? And look, there's a statue of Julini here too. But this one's different. This one is wearing a wedding dress.

JULINI: Laila...

LAILA: Oh my god, the statue can speak.

JULINI: Laila Majenun, I'm not a statue. I am Julini.

LAILA: Julini? I never would have thought.... What are you doing here?

JULINI: Because I'm dead. Are you?

LAILA: Yeah, me too. Oh, I've missed you so much! But you look great! What's that eye shadow you're using?

JULINI: How is it on earth? How is Roima? Doing well?

LAILA: And your nail polish matches you lipstick! Is it imported?

JULINI: Of course it's imported. How did you know?

            (*Suddenly, a million butterflies fly closer.*)

            Look, so many butterflies! But, but wait, they're not butterflies. That's Ike, and Esyi, and Syeni, and Wanda, and Téa... Are they all dead too?

IKE: Julini, Julini we're here. (*Falling*) Ouch.... That was a bad landing. Look, there's Laila.

TÉA: Oh Laila, Laila, I've missed you so much. (*Embracing LAILA*) I'm so happy to see you again.

            (TÉA *embraces* LAILA *and then they all run around greeting one another. The atmosphere becomes one of gaiety with much giggling.*)

IKE: Are we dead or not? I don't see any difference?

JULINI: I don't know. What I do know is that I'm stuck here. It's like the opposite of being with a john who's all hot and bothered but you're not in the mood and keeping your legs tightly crossed. Now your legs are wide open but he's keeping his zipper closed.

Do you see that, those two doors? One is for men, one is for women. I can go in they tell me but only if I go through the men's door. But I'm a woman. I don't want to.

WANDA: Well just go through. What's stopping you?

JULINI: You try!

(WANDA *saunters to the door for women and tries to go through but a million rays of light strike her and she is thrown out.*)

WANDA: Owwww. What the hell?

GUARD 2: Your name is Masdrai Djuheri, shot dead.

WANDA: My name is Wanda, dear boy. That guy whose name you just mentioned was buried long ago. I am Wanda.

JULINI: So that's the way it goes. They refuse us.

IKE: I want to try.

ALL OTHER TRANSWOMEN: (*Together*) Me too, me too…

(*All of the other* TRANSWOMEN *try at once to go through the women's door but again lightning strikes and they are thrown out. They all scream in pain.*)

GUARD 2: Kemaliau Atmodjo, shot dead.... Aklis Suryapala, shot dead.... Lie Chin Ming, shot dead.... Raden Sutomor, shot dead.... Boedi Indrapaksa, shot dead…

(*And on and on, with the sound like an echo.*)

JULINI: See how it feels? You still want to go in? You like being shocked like that? If you don't want to get a shock, you can go through the men's door. They're sure to let you in. But I won't do it. I am a woman. I've chosen to be a woman and so I must be allowed to go through the women's door. If they reject me, so be it. I will wait here until I am accepted. It's up to you to do what you want.

IKE: Isn't there any other way?

JULINI: No, there's not. That's why I have chosen to go on silent strike.

ESYI: A silent strike? What do you mean? Not moving or anything? Like a statue?

JULINI: Yes.

SYENI: How many years will that be?

JULINI: Until they let us go through the gateway that's right for us.

WANDA: How are you going to stay silent like that—not move or anything? In the morning, there's at least one part of my body that moves on its own, whether I want it to or not.

IKE: You dope. That's not what she's talking about. I agree with Julini. We'll go on strike. Don't worry; I'm sure we can do it.

Haven't you heard that story about that country whose public representatives are able to stay silent and do nothing for four whole years? If they can do it, I'm sure we can too. When do we begin, Jul.

JULINI: Now if you'd like.

(Music begins to play and all the TRANSWOMEN *begin to sing "The Trans Song.")*

ALL: *Who says we are trash*
We are diamonds in the gutter
Who said our lives are meaningless
How silent the world would be without us

There is night and there is day
There is up and there is down
There is man and there is woman
And we are right in the middle

(*As the music is playing but before the* TRANSWOMEN *begin to sing, the* OFFICIAL, *who is wearing a blindfold, is led by his* WIFE *to the* MINISTER *of Home Affairs.*)

OFFICIAL: There you have it, Minister. That is what I have to report: I failed. The unrest broke out during my watch. Even though it was put down in the end, the responsibility is still on my shoulders. I am not longer able to serve as this city's highest official. This is my letter of resignation.

WIFE: It's just lucky I was there, Minister. If not, this city would still be in a mess. We were able to wipe out the gang of criminals. Unfortunately, their ringleaders managed to get away. But for now, at least, the city is safe, sir. I too am responsible for my husband's affairs. You might even say I am his backbone. Without me, the situation would be difficult, to say the least.

MINISTER: Excellent, that's excellent. Such is the way a good wife should be. And you, sir, I reject your letter of resignation outright. In fact, we have prepared a medal for you as well as a raise in your position. There is no better candidate than you. Take care of this city well.

OFFICIAL: Oh god, that's it for me...

WIFE: Thank you, Minister.

LIGHTS CHANGE

(BLEKI *is visible, running around in confusion.*)

BLEKI: Boss.... Tibal.... Where are you, boss? Where are you, boss, where are you? (*Disappears.*)

(SAWIL *and* BILUN *pass by quickly.*)

BILUN: I think we'd best trade in used bottles or cardboard boxes. We don't have enough money to buy a country.

SAWIL: Don't be so weak minded. You got to be strong. Once a super trader, always a super trader. Don't worry about money. We can print as much money as we want. But we have to go to the auction fast. Otherwise someone will beat us first. The country we're looking to contact is very cheap. We must do whatever is necessary to make it ours. (*Leaves.*)

BILUN: We don't have any money. We're dirt poor. We eat from the trash cans at restaurants but want to buy a country? Sawil, Sawil, wait for me.

(BILUN *exits following* SAWIL. *The* TRANSWOMEN *begin to sing with great fervor, "We are Guinea Pigs."*)

TRANSWOMEN: *We are guinea pigs*
    Objects for research
    Objects for those in power
    Tortured souls, everlasting wounds

    But we are human
    Not lice and not dogs
    We want to sleep in peace
    To live in peace with others

    That is our hope
    Hopefully to be realized soon
    For none of this
    Is any of our doing

LIGHTS CHANGE

Closure

Somewhere, everywhere. ROIMA *appears alone under a purple light and begins to sing "Roima's Wish." The other characters emerge and sing along.)*

ALL: *The earth and the sky*
      Clear and calm
      Death or life
      Just so there is closure

      All of this unrest
      Has its basis in greed
      Hunting and hunted by
      Emptiness

      (They then sing "Julini's Wish.")

      My life is full of meaning
      I know my movements
      And in death hunting whom

      I am not an empty barrel
      My chest is ready to explode
      With my love for you, Roima

      (Now they sing "Everyone's Hope.")

      Everyone searches for meaning
      But all they find is clouds
      Everyone searches for love
      But what they find is only disappointment
      Everyone searches for happiness
      But all they find is emptiness

      (Lights illuminate the sky.)

THE END

Biographical Information

Norbertus "Nano" Riantiarno (June 6, 1949–January 20, 2023) was an Indonesian actor, director, and playwright. Born in Cirebon, West Java, Riantiarno began his career in theater while still in high school, after graduation from which he moved to Jakarta to attend ATNI, the Indonesian National Theater Academy (Akademi Teater Nasional Indonesia). There, he met Teguh Karya, a leading theater director, and assisted Karya in the founding of the troupe Teater Populer, where he continued to practice acting under Karya's leadership. While working with Karya, Riantiarno performed in several plays and films. In 1971, he began enrolled at the Driyakara School of Philosophy, and in 1975 he left Teater Populer to travel throughout the archipelago and study various forms of traditional Indonesian theater. At the completion of his travels, Riantiarno and several other theater workers, including his future wife, Ratna Madjid, founded Teater Koma on March 1, 1977. The title of the troupe was drawn from Riantiarno's belief that theater is a journey without periods but one filled with commas.

Between the time of its founding and Riantiarno's death, Teater Koma staged 225 productions, many of them with explicit political content and a number of which were banned during the "New Order" period of government, one of them being *Cockroach Opera*. Even with increased reformation of Indonesia's political system following the fall of Soeharto in 1998, Riantiarno continued to pepper his plays with political messages and his plays continued to attract a large and loyal audience.

John H McGlynn, originally from Wisconsin, U.S.A., is a long-term resident of Indonesia, having lived in Jakarta almost continually since 1976. A graduate of the University of Michigan Ann Arbor (1981), with a Masters degree in Indonesian language and literature, he is the translator of several dozen book-length publications, both under his own name and his penname, Willem Samuels. His dozens of book-length translations of Indonesian literary work have garnered much international praise.

Through the Lontar Foundation, which he co-founded in 1987, McGlynn has ushered into print close to 250 books on Indonesian literature and culture. Also through Lontar, he initiated the "On the Record" film documentation program which has thus far produced more than fifty films on Indonesian writers and more than thirty films on Indonesian oral traditions.

McGlynn is the Indonesian country editor for several foreign literary journals. He is a member of the Association of Asian Studies and a founding member of both the Asia Pacific Writers and Translators Association and the 17,000 Islands of Imagination Foundation. He is an emeritus trustee of AMINEF, the American Indonesian Exchange Foundation, which oversees the Fulbright scholarship program in Indonesia.

Barbara Hatley taught Indonesian Studies for many years at Monash University, then moved as Professor of Indonesian to the University of Tasmania, where she now holds a Professor Emeritus position. Her major research interests are in Indonesian performing arts, modern literature, and gender studies.

Barbara's publications include *Javanese Performances on an Indonesian Stage Contesting Culture, Embracing Change* (NUS Press, 2008), *Theatre and Performance in the Asia Pacific: Regional Modernities in the Global Era*, co-authored with Denise Varney, Peter Eckersall, and Chris Hudson, and *Performing Contemporary Indonesia: Celebrating Identity, Constructing Community* edited with Brett Hough. She has also published book chapters and journal articles on gender issues such as "Postcoloniality and the Feminine in Modern Indonesian Literature" in Tony Day and Keith Foulcher (eds.) *Clearing a Space: Postcolonial Readings of Modern Indonesian Literature* and "Hearing Women's Voices, Contesting Women's Bodies in Post-New Order Indonesia" in *Intersections: Gender and Sexuality in Asia and the Pacific*.

While teaching at Monash, Barbara staged performances of Indonesian plays with her students for which she translated the plays into English. This includes her translation of *Bom Waktu* (Time Bomb) by Nano Riantiarno, which first appeared in Lontar's 1992 publication, *Time Bomb and Cockroach Opera*.